THE
EXPEDITIONA

Sorry I have not written
long time. no doubt she he
getting on. I should have
been so busy always
hardly any time share
of health at present the
I We had a good voyage
was very calm. I think
the up the line tomorrow so it i
you my proper address. I shall see
Ethel as soon as I can

TO G
Y
GP
A Har

LETTERS
from the
TRENCHES

LETTERS
from the
TRENCHES

A Soldier of the Great War

BILL LAMIN

MICHAEL O'MARA BOOKS LIMITED

First published in Great Britain in 2009 by
Michael O'Mara Books Limited
9 Lion Yard
Tremadoc Road
London SW4 7NQ

The illustration on the half-title page shows a cap badge of the
York and Lancaster Regiment from the Great War
(York and Lancaster Regimental Museum, Rotherham)

Papers used by Michael O'Mara Books Limited are natural, recyclable products
made from wood grown in sustainable forests. The manufacturing processes
conform to the environmental regulations of the country of origin.

A CIP catalogue record for this book is available from the British Library

ISBN: 978-1-84317-373-1

1 3 5 7 9 10 8 6 4 2

www.mombooks.com

Designed and typeset by Design 23

Printed and bound in Finland by WS Bookwell, Juva

CONTENTS

To the memory of
Harry Lamin and his comrades of
the Great War

PREFACE

HARRY LAMIN WAS AN unexceptional man who lived through the exceptional horrors of the First World War. Through his letters from that time we can gain some insight into the fate of the ordinary soldier – for Harry was a private soldier for the whole of his service. The letters are not sensational. The style is limited and often rather flat, but somehow the character of the man is immediately accessible. Online readers have commented that they feel that they know Harry personally; as his saga progressed on the Internet, some came to feel that they had gained an extra member of their own family. He was my grandfather.

The source of the material seems to fascinate many people. There is no great mystery, however, no exciting, sudden discovery. One drawer of a desk at my parents' home housed old family documents, photographs of long-forgotten relatives, newspaper cuttings and the like. I was around eleven or twelve years old when I first became aware that Harry's letters were in that desk drawer. I suspect that they had been recovered and placed in the desk when Ethel, Harry's wife, died. They were in no particular order, just bundled together in the drawer. I don't think that I read any of them until a little later, but I can remember, aged around sixteen, being fascinated by his letter of 6 October 1917 to his brother Jack, in which he describes beating off a German attack and 'did not feel nervous when I saw them coming over'.

Once I'd claimed the letters, after my sister Anita and I had cleared the family home, I did little with them for months. Eventually, I took them into the comprehensive school where I worked to see whether teachers in the History Department could use them for pupils studying the First World War. Their response was very enthusiastic. A book was suggested, but the amount of work required to get the letters and other material into a suitable form was daunting, especially as I was holding down a demanding teaching job. Then, of course, there was no guarantee that a publisher would be interested.

The idea of creating a blog from the letters was a wonderful inspiration. Researching the use of blogs for the schoolchildren

(I was Head of IT), I made the connection between the letters and the (then) accepted format for a blog. I realized that I could use the Internet to 'time shift' and publish the letters in precisely the same timescale as that in which my grandfather had written them. In this I was lucky: not only was 2007 exactly ninety years after Harry Lamin was first sent to the front, but the days of the week in 1917 fell on the same days in 2007 – so Harry's letter of Wednesday, 7 February 1917 was published on Wednesday, 7 February 2007. Readers of the blog could experience the same anxieties that had confronted Harry's family back in 1917 and 1918. They wouldn't know when the next letter would appear. They would have no idea whether Harry was all right, or had become a casualty – perhaps even been killed. Crucially, I only had to deal with one letter at a time – quite manageable.

The photographs that had surfaced with the letters proved to be an important element of the blog. In fact, there were only two photographs of Harry up to the end of the war in 1918: the Awsworth Board School photograph of him as a child among his classmates and teachers, and the picture of him with his squad that was almost certainly taken when he was first conscripted. From each of these I doubled up the photographs by cropping individual images of Harry from the groups. When I started the blog in the summer of 2006, however, I had only the photograph from the school taken in the early 1890s. I had no knowledge of the squad picture showing Harry in uniform.

I had been posting on the blog for about a year when my sister turned up the dog-eared photograph from a box of 'bits' left over from the house clearance. That picture is crucial to the blog. An image of Harry the soldier made it much easier for readers to identify with Harry the man. As soon as the distressed picture was published, readers with expertise in photograph manipulation offered to 'do their best' to restore it. The results were pleasing, sharpening the image and removing the blemishes that had defaced the original.

The first posts to the blog introduced Harry and described his background and family. The idea was to see whether I could generate a little interest before the 'live' letters started appearing. On 7 February 2007, exactly ninety years after it was written, I posted on the blog a transcript of Harry's first letter from the training camp in Rugeley, Staffordshire. After that, each of his letters appeared on the same date on which it had been written, albeit nine decades earlier. Those reading on the web could see his story, his war, unfold as though it were happening now.

Since the launch, the success of the blog has been astonishing. What had started as a hobby has grown into a worldwide phenomenon. The 'real-time' serialization of Private Harry Lamin's letters has attracted well over 2 million page loads and drawn media attention from the press, television and radio around the world. It has gained a devoted set of readers, anxiously checking the blog to find out what was happening to Harry ninety years earlier. 'I check for a Harry letter before I check my own emails,' was a typical response. Readers seemed to identify with this man from ninety years ago, and frequently added words of encouragement over events taking place in a completely different time frame. The neatest analogy came from a reader who reminded me that we look up at the stars and observe events that happened thousands, if not millions, of years ago, and yet we accept them without question as 'now' events.

The blog became such an event, not only for those who followed it, but for me as well. As soon as we started to read the letters, we would be transported back to another era, feeling, even sharing, the anxiety that Harry's family would have felt so many years earlier.

In this book, as on the Internet, the transcriptions of Harry's letters are as faithful and as accurate as possible. Harry's grammar and spelling are not always perfect, but still reflect great credit on the education he received at Awsworth Board School. State schooling at that time (for those not educated privately) was compulsory, but generally limited to around four years of drilling in the 'three Rs' – 'Reading, wRiting and 'Rithmetic'. The quality of his letters – especially since his schooling ended when he was thirteen – would certainly bear comparison with the efforts of the pupils I teach today – National Curriculum, SATS, myriad 'initiatives' and all.

Again as on the blog, I have tried to be a little selective in the choice of letters that appear here. There is a fair amount of repetition in them, and not all contribute a great deal. Similarly, the war diary of Harry's battalion, the tersely worded daily account of the activities of the unit, contributes much to our understanding of the experiences of Harry and of other 'ordinary' soldiers but, in its listing of everyday occurrences, would become tedious if reproduced as a complete document.

It is useful, I think, to stress the most important aspect of the blog. 'World War I – Experiences of an English Soldier' (http://wwar1. blogspot.com), to which this book is a companion, attracted attention and followers through the unique feature of the publication of the letters in 'real time plus ninety years', each being posted on to the Internet exactly ninety years to the day after Harry wrote it. The only way of determining what was what was going on in his life was to wait for the next letter. There were, too, some significant gaps which worried many readers, since they had no way of discovering whether Harry lived, was wounded or had been killed in action. The next post might well have been a standard letter or telegram from the War Office giving Ethel, his wife, terrible news. My instruction for visitors to the website simply read: 'To find Harry's fate, follow the blog.' There was no other way for them to learn what happened to him.

Even on the blog, the journey towards the finishing line – the end of the war – was not quite as effective for readers because the date on which the fighting ended is well known (something denied to Harry at the time, of course). Questions were asked about whether I would give an account of Harry's life after the war. Naturally, to maintain the suspense, I could give no indication that he would survive, and had to ignore the questions.

The extent and seriousness of the involvement of readers of Harry's blog is probably best reflected in the comments made. To date (the blog continues as I write) there have been over 1,500 comments posted by people who have followed it (enough for a separate book – wwar1comments.blogspot.com). The support, appreciation and intense engagement that became so evident have been extraordinary. In the whole collection of comments, I can remember but two that were slightly critical; the rest, in total, made all the hard work well worthwhile.

BILL LAMIN
February 2009

CHAPTER I

HARRY AND FAMILY – BEFORE CONSCRIPTION, 28 DECEMBER 1916

WILLIAM HENRY BONSER – HARRY – LAMIN was born on 28 August 1887 in Awsworth, Nottinghamshire, close to the border with Derbyshire. I have a little documented information about his childhood, and some family hearsay. If I recount all that I have discovered, readers can complete their own picture of the boy that grew up to be Private Harry Lamin.

His family had originally been well-to-do farmers, but in 1875 sold up the farm in Annesley and moved to nearby Awsworth. I have a beautiful poster advertising the farm sale. The family tale is that drink was involved in the decline of Henry Lamin's farm. Subsequently, according to the 1881 and 1891 census data, Henry, Harry's father, then became a farm labourer, later a 'chemical labourer'. A menial job in the chemical industry at the end of the nineteenth century would not have been too overburdened by 'Health-and-Safety' issues, but Henry lived on until April 1918, when he died, aged seventy-three.

At some time before quitting the farm, Henry had married Sarah Bonser (hence Harry's unusual name). There were five children who survived to school age: John (Jack) was born in 1870, Sarah Anne (Annie) in 1874, Catherine (Kate) in 1877, and Harry ten years later, in 1887. A third daughter, Mary Esther was born in 1872, but had died, aged seventeen, when Harry was two, and so has no active part in this account.

Harry's mother, Sarah, appears on the 1881 census but has disappeared by 1891, the family Bible recording that she died in 1889, while a card printed for her funeral records the date as 13 March 1891, when she was forty-three. Harry therefore lost his mother, as well as an older sister, at a very early age. He was probably brought up by his grandmother, with whom the family lived after the farm was sold, and perhaps also by Jack, his brother, some seventeen years his senior, and by his sisters Annie and Kate.

Harry's class at Awsworth Board School, c. 1894; he is third from left in the second row.

We know that Harry attended Awsworth Board School, as did his brother and sisters. The photograph of Harry as a youngster is taken from his school photograph: he is third from the left in the second row from the front. Unfortunately, there is no date for the photograph, but he looks about seven so it must have been taken around 1894. Both the school and the wall seen behind the children are still there, although the latter has been modified to allow vehicles to enter and use the former playground as a car park. The old school is still a fine building and is now used by a packaging-design company.

My family still has books and cross-stitch samplers used or stitched by Mary Esther, Annie and Kate while they were at the same school, and I have to assume that Jack too would have received his early education in the same establishment as his brothers and sisters. We must commend the efforts of the teachers. Although his schooling ended when he was thirteen, Harry writes a fine letter with sound, if not quite perfect, grammar and spelling.

Jack became a distinguished clergyman, while Kate trained as a midwife and, later, became a matron in the main hospital in the City of Leeds, Leeds General Infirmary.

In the 1901 census, Harry, aged thirteen, is found to be staying with his older brother in Cowley, Oxford. Jack was then a schoolmaster (in the 1891 census, he is listed as an assistant schoolmaster in Awsworth). I have no way of knowing whether this was a short visit for Harry, or a longer stay, but I suspect the latter, for Oxford people and places are mentioned in his letters. With no mother at home, this may well have been a convenient arrangement, reducing the strain on the family's finances.

Later, Harry worked in one of the many local lace factories near Ilkeston, Derbyshire, living at 19 Mill Street in that town, in a terraced house that still exists. In 1914 he gave his occupation on his marriage certificate as 'lacemaker', but I believe that he was actually a maintenance fitter (mechanic) for lace-making machines.

The most common occupations for men in Ilkeston then were coal miner or working at the local Stanton Iron Works: a job in a lace factory would have been seen as a relatively 'soft' option. At the time, Ilkeston was in a heavily industrialized region of England, principally coal mining and its associated industries, among them the large iron and steel works. Both industries have declined, and indeed virtually disappeared, in my lifetime – that is, since the 1950s. During the Great War, however, they were at peak production, the war itself producing an enormous demand for coal and steel.

In the various letters and accounts by or concerning Harry Lamin, several characters play an important part, and it seems useful to introduce them at this point. First of all, the two principal recipients of Harry's letters.

Catherine (Kate) was the next youngest after Harry, but even so was still ten years older than him. According to the 1901 census, she was still at home at twenty-four years of age, with no recorded occupation. What we know now, but which would have been – indeed was – kept very quiet at the time, is that Kate had an illegitimate daughter, born in 1910. Connie – Constance Wilkinson Lamin – became an important element in Harry's home life.

By the time that Harry was conscripted into the Army in 1917, Kate had become a successful midwife in London. I have a range of certificates and letters of commendation from her time there. In late 1917, Harry's letters indicate that she had moved to Leeds, where she eventually became a matron at Leeds General Infirmary. Her flat in Hanover Square, Leeds, still exists and looks, today, a very pleasant place to live. She continued in her profession after the end of the war, only, like so many of her contemporaries, to find herself caught up in another war in 1939. She died in July 1948, when she was seventy years old. My older sister, Anita, remembers her as a 'formidable woman'; she never married.

The oldest of Henry and Sarah Lamin's children, John Ernest (Jack) Lamin, was born in 1870, seventeen years before his brother Harry. As mentioned earlier, the 1901 census shows that he was then an elementary schoolmaster living in Oxford. By the time Harry began to write to him from the front, however, Jack had

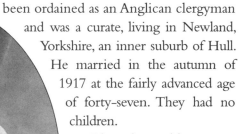

been ordained as an Anglican clergyman and was a curate, living in Newland, Yorkshire, an inner suburb of Hull. He married in the autumn of 1917 at the fairly advanced age of forty-seven. They had no children.

I have been able to trace some of his career after the war. Coincidentally, he was to spend some time at Rugeley in Staffordshire, where Harry did his basic

Kate Lamin as a young nurse.

training for the Army. He eventually became a canon (in this case, an honorary appointment in the Church of England, for senior, well-respected members of the clergy) attached to the Minster at York, where I understand there is a memorial plaque to him.

Connie (Constance Wilkinson Lamin) was, initially, something of a mystery. She was brought up by Harry and his wife, Ethel, as an older sister to their son Willie, but she certainly wasn't his real sister.

Willie, my father (whose memory, at the age of ninety-three, is no longer very reliable), has said that Connie was the daughter of a wealthy family in the town. As she was what we would now call disabled, these rich folks advertised in the local newspaper for someone to look after her. Ethel, Harry's wife, answered the advert and brought up Connie as her own. This was the 'official' family story to cover up the embarrassing truth that Connie was actually Kate's illegitimate daughter. The birth certificate I have obtained confirms this; it may be that the 'Wilkinson' part of her name came from the father, but if so, he did not stay to help raise her.

It is difficult, now, to comprehend just what social and moral stigma was attached to illegitimacy in the first half – at least – of the twentieth century, or the lengths to which people would sometimes go to conceal such a birth. In an age when religious faith and regular churchgoing were the norms rather than, as now, exceptions, to bear a child out of wedlock all too frequently resulted in social ostracism – or worse – quite often at the hands of other family members. Then, too, contraception was uncertain

Connie, the 'daughter' raised as their own by Harry and his wife.

even if it were available, and abortion highly illegal, resulting in desperate women finding themselves in the hands of unscrupulous and dangerous back-street practitioners. Little wonder, then, that Kate and her family chose to conceal Connie's parentage. At least she was loved.

At that time, and quite apart from the disapproval she would have faced from many quarters, Kate would not have been able to pursue her successful career in nursing with a daughter in tow, and so it must have been – and was – very convenient for Ethel to take over the raising of Connie, while everyone in the know conspired to keep the truth of her parentage secret. It is likely that Kate helped Harry's family through the difficult years during and following the Great War. If her daughter were living with Harry and Ethel, that would make a good deal of sense.

As mentioned before, Connie was physically handicapped. She had cerebral palsy, a condition that usually occurs at birth. It may be that Kate, a midwife, tried to deliver her own child and suffered complications, but I have no information. Letters mention Connie 'walking', an odd reference to an unremarkable feat in a child that only made sense when I received her death certificate, which confirmed that she had suffered from cerebral palsy.

The photograph on page 159 is of her and Willie, and since she was born in 1910, she was probably about eight when it was taken. Willie would have been two. Connie's stance in the photograph apparently confirms the diagnosis of cerebral palsy and her consequent walking difficulties. Sadly, she died, aged nineteen, in 1929, and was buried on Christmas Eve in Ilkeston cemetery. Nearly twenty years later, Kate was buried beside her daughter, and only child, in the same grave. It is quite clear from his letters that Harry doted on Connie, and fretted about her condition.

Harry's wife, born Ethel Watson, was a local Ilkeston girl, the daughter of a plumber. They married in March 1914 in a civil ceremony in the register office in Basford, a suburb of Nottingham. As has been said, Harry's occupation was recorded as 'lacemaker', while Ethel was simply listed as 'spinster'. Their wedding took place some five months before the outbreak of war, a war about which Ethel never wanted to speak after Harry's return from the front. She died in 1964, when I was in my teens. I remember her as a kindly, no-nonsense woman who made an amazingly creamy mashed potato.

William Lamin (Willie), my father, was born to Harry and Ethel in March 1916, two years after they had wed and almost a year before Harry joined up to fight. He grew up in Ilkeston and was a noted soloist, first as a boy soprano and then as a tenor, in the church choir for an astonishing seventy-five years. He became a successful textile salesman, and had a brush with the military in the Second World War, apparently missing being shipped to Singapore, and almost certain capture or death, by minutes. His transfer

Harry's wife – and the author's grandmother – Ethel Lamin.

to the Army Physical Training (APT) Corps in Aldershot came through as he was on parade, ready to embark with the rest of his unit for Singapore. He was fortunate to spend the duration of the war as a PT instructor, remaining in England, for in February 1942, shortly after his draft arrived in Singapore, the allegedly impregnable fortress island fell to the Japanese, so completing their lightning conquest of Malaya.

There was another son, Arthur, born in 1914. I have a baptismal certificate from the parish church in Ilkeston. No one alive can recall any mention of Arthur, and I assumed that he died in infancy. After a helpful reader identified the record of his death I was able to confirm that he did indeed die as an infant.

Willie (now known as Bill) is, as I write, still alive at ninety-three and living in a nursing home in Derbyshire. Harry frequently mentions Willie in his letters, underlining what a terrible wrench it must have been to leave behind a baby son to go to the privations and horrors of the war.

Willie knew Jack – his Uncle John – quite well, and always refers to him in a respectful manner. Jack was considered to be one of the successful members of the family, and officiated at Willie's wedding to Nancy Elizabeth Satterthwaite in 1941.

Sarah Anne disappeared from the family records quite early on in my researches, and I had assumed that she had died, like her sister, Mary Esther. I later discovered, however, that Annie (as Harry refers to her in his letters) also had an illegitimate child, named George. He too served in the First World War and at some time afterwards emigrated to Australia. Annie later married – Harry's letters make several references to her wedding – and lived to a ripe old age. I have now realized that she was my own 'Auntie' Annie whom I sometimes spent days with as a toddler in Ilkeston. I can just remember her death in 1953, aged seventy-nine, when I was five.

These then are the main characters in Harry Lamin's world, names that occur again and again in his letters. It is now time to turn to the man himself.

CHAPTER 2

PREPARING FOR WAR, FEBRUARY – MAY 1917

HARRY, ETHEL AND THEIR nine-month-old son Willie received a Christmas message from the War Office in late December 1916. At twenty-nine and not in a reserved occupation (that is, a job considered vital to the war effort; those in reserved occupations were exempted from military service), Harry must have known that conscription was inevitable and imminent. The call-up papers would not have come as a surprise to him, although married men were not obliged to be called up until May 1916. By then, after more than two years of war and hundreds of thousands of casualties, the Army was facing a manpower shortage, for the flood of volunteers had all but dried up.

Harry duly enlisted on 28 December 1916. He would have been given a rail warrant to take him to Rugeley Camp, on the eastern edge of Cannock Chase, in Staffordshire, where he was to commence his basic training, prior to selecting, or being assigned to, a regiment or corps.

The extent and scale of that camp needs to be appreciated. A contemporary map shows around five hundred huts, eighteen parade grounds, a hospital and the railway branch line which connected the camp to the main line. With around twenty-five soldiers to a hut, the camp would have had a capacity of 12,500 men. That seems an enormous figure, until we realize that, not quite six months earlier, more than that number of British troops had been killed before breakfast on the first day of the Battle of the Somme, 1 July 1916. Many units would still have been short of men, even by December; some battalions had been shelled and machine-gunned virtually out of existence. In extreme cases they had been disbanded, and their remaining officers and other ranks assigned to other units. Rugeley Camp was there to satisfy the endless need for fresh replacements.

Harry would have travelled to Rugeley by train. Because the whole of the East Midlands was heavily industrialized, there was a concentration of railways, run by separate, private companies. As a result, there would have been an almost endless number of ways by which Harry could have travelled from his home to Rugeley. There were three railway stations in Ilkeston alone, one within a few hundred yards of his home, and two in Rugeley, with branch line that served the Army camp running about two miles (just over 3km)

Rugeley Training Camp in Staffordshire, as it was in 1917.

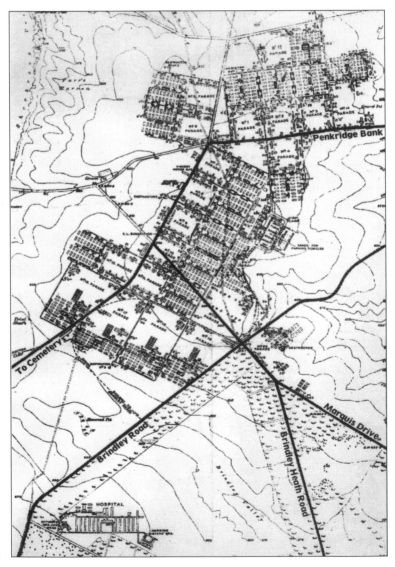

outside the town. Harry would have arrived, with a trainload of other conscripts, most unsure of what he was to face.

The camp was effectively a production line for soldiers. On arrival, Harry would have had his details checked, undergone a medical inspection and been kitted out, and would then have put on his new uniform for a squad photograph. Then he would have started basic training, which consisted of much 'square bashing' (eighteen parade grounds!) and physical training (PT). The general form would be recognized by any soldier who has joined up in the last ninety years. There would also have been classes in aspects of military training, and, for some conscripts, in even more basic education.

Amazingly, Harry's squad photograph from Rugeley has survived, although I was not aware of its existence until the summer of 2007, a year after the Internet version of this account was started. The picture turned up in a box of miscellaneous items at my sister Anita's home. There are two versions now: the original print, faded, much battered and creased after ninety years of obscurity and neglect, and a second version that has been subjected to modern computer technology to 'clean up' the image and remove the worst signs of wear and tear (the photo had obviously been folded up quite small at one point).

Harry, who is at the right-hand end the front row (see next page), has his belt on upside down (or, just possibly, all the other conscripts have their belts upside down). This confirms that he must have only recently received his uniform and kit, for a few parades would have made sure that he got the belt right, drill sergeants being what they are. After my own, very limited, military training, there is still no way, forty years on, that I can wear any

belt with the buckle on the right. It just feels wrong.

The photograph also shows the considerable range of ages among the squad. Harry, at twenty-nine, certainly doesn't look the oldest. One of the recruits has a wristwatch, a relatively new kind of timepiece that was much more useful in a trench than a pocket watch, but which would have been quite an expensive item for a private soldier. On first seeing the photograph I wondered whether the building with the stained-glass window in the background might still exist, but a quick look at satellite images on the Internet showed that today, there is hardly a trace of the original camp at Rugeley left. A recent newspaper article described how a replica of an original wooden hut had just been installed there as a museum piece.

Harry would not have been at the camp for much more than a month when, on Wednesday, 7 February 1917, he wrote the first of his war letters to have survived, to his sister Kate.

37/74, M Coy, 15 Hut, 10th Training Reserves, Rugeley, Staffs
February 7th 1917

Dear Kate
I was very pleased to receive your letter. The weather here is very cold and we don't get much fire. We have been vaccinated this week well

Left: The squad photograph, after enhancement to remove the creases and marks. Harry is at far right in the front row.

Right: The letter to Kate, with its envelope, which is franked 'Rugeley Camp'.

last Monday but we have to do all drills just the same. Ethel says Annie's cold is much better. I can't get a shut of mine but I am lucky to keep as well as I do. We have four blankets a piece and a bag of straw about 6in. from the floor on three planks to lie on. There are 29 in our hut and there only suppose to have twenty. I think it will be another five or six weeks before I get a pass I am ready for one anytime. Ethel says Connie and Willie are alright he will soon be a year old now and have two letters from Jack he seems to be getting on all right. We don't get too much to eat, bread and jam dripping we have to do the cleaning in turns but the cooking is done at the cookhouse. I have not got any fatter yet I don't suppose I shall do

Will write soon
With Love from
Harry

Interior of a training-camp hut, c. 1917. The 'bag of straw . . . on three planks' on which the men slept can be seen at right; the stove and its chimney are at left.

A recent drawing showing the construction of the type of hut only too familiar to Harry.

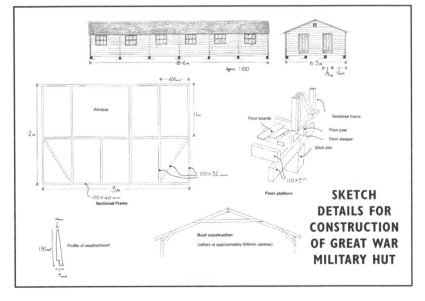

SKETCH DETAILS FOR CONSTRUCTION OF GREAT WAR MILITARY HUT

The letter tells us a great deal. The troops lived in wooden huts. Each hut was about 60 feet (18 metres) long by 16 feet (5 metres) wide, with a cast-iron stove in the middle which would have provided the only heating. The straw palliasse on planks would have been a poor substitute for Harry's bed at home, and he would certainly have needed the four blankets to keep warm, for the winter of 1917 was bitterly cold, and the huts draughty and lacking insulation.

In time, the Army would replace many of its wooden huts with the corrugated-steel prefabricated Nissen hut, invented by a Canadian officer in 1916 and used in the First World War and, extensively, in the Second. At Rugeley in 1917, however, twenty-nine men in a hut designed for twenty illustrates the pressure to turn out replacement soldiers for the front line.

Vaccinations – soldiers were inoculated against typhoid and paratyphoid on joining up. Whatever the controversy today over the use of vaccines, the insanitary conditions and poor hygiene of the trenches made such protection not just reasonable, but essential. Also available at the time was an anti-tetanus injection. However, this was generally administered after injury rather than as a preventive measure.

The 'pass' Harry refers to would have allowed him a short leave at the end of the training period, prior to joining his unit on active service, probably across the Channel in France or Belgium.

'Dripping' is the residue of fat and juices that is left after meat has been roasted, poured into a bowl and allowed to cool and set, to be used again for frying or roasting. Before cholesterol and salt were identified as mainly harmful, 'bread and dripping' was a common snack, or even meal, in the industrial Midlands of England and elsewhere. I can remember enjoying it in the 1950s. The fat from the Sunday joint, with the wonderful brown jelly underneath it, was spread on to bread with a liberal amount of salt, and the slice then eaten. It had the merit of being full of flavour, cheap and quite nutritious, although probably not very healthy.

In general, it would appear that the newly joined conscripts were not particularly well fed. The last line of the letter sums up Harry's feelings with a touch of wry humour. We shall hear more of his experiences of Army food – always a preoccupation of soldiers – as his service progresses.

The War Office specified the period of training for volunteer infantrymen in 1914 and 1915 as eight months. By the time Harry, a conscript, started his training, the desperate need for soldiers had reduced this period to around five months. Perhaps this reduction was not really a problem, as no amount of training could prepare these young men sent to the front line for what was to follow.

As an extra detail at Rugeley at this time, the Army had built a replica of the Messines–Wytschaete Ridge in Belgian Flanders on the camp's training grounds on Cannock Chase. The actual ridge lies a few miles to the south of the town of Ypres (Ieper), and in early 1917 was occupied by the Germans in well dug-in emplacements; Ypres itself was held by the British, who also occupied a 'salient' jutting eastwards from the town into German-held territory. The ridge was only a few metres high, but it was sufficiently prominent to dominate the plain, giving excellent views of the Allies' movements and dispositions. For months, the British High Command had been making preparations to take this ridge, in order to deprive the Germans of their commanding view over the Ypres Salient. The mock-up on Cannock Chase was just a small part of the meticulous planning that went into the operation. For Harry, the Messines Ridge was to be a significant element of his experiences over the next month or so.

By May 1917, with his basic training completed, Harry was in France with an infantry battalion to which he had been assigned, from where he wrote both to his brother and to one of his sisters. Harry's references in his letters to his location on the Western Front were always to France or, occasionally, Flanders (an area that in fact occupies parts of France, Belgium and Holland). He would have actually spent most of his time in Belgium, but that small country, so important in the history of the Great War, never gets a mention.

Shortly after crossing the Channel, Harry wrote to his brother Jack.

Dear Jack

Just a line to let you know I am alright and that I have landed in France. The weather here has been very hot. Not at all a bad sort of place. There is a pretty town about two miles away on the coast but it is out of bounds. This is my address we have got to put it in the middle of our letter. I don't know why. 33502 Pt Lamin West York Reg [West Yorkshire Regiment] number lines 33rd IBDAPO section 17 BEF France. No doubt you have read about the Arcadian going down. Well the draft to Mesopotamia which I should've been on had it not been for my teeth, was on it. I have heard from one that was on it. he was in the same hut as me at Rugely. I think they were about all saved. Write as soon as you get this letter as I should be going up the line of next week and perhaps get to a different regiment so write soon.

yours truly

Harry.

Is there some anticipation, perhaps even apprehension, at the prospect of 'going up the line'? Nor do I know why, regarding the address, 'we have got to put it in the middle of our letter'. Clearly it was not an enduring instruction, for it rarely appeared there again in Harry's letters.

At that time, soldiers' numbers were regimental numbers, so that, changing regiment meant being issued with a new number. (In the British Army today, an individual soldier's number is his unique Army number, and remains constant for the whole of his service.) Harry's number, given in this first letter from France, didn't last long, as he changed regiment – having previously been assigned to two others, from which he had rapidly been moved. I have not been able to discover what process was involved in assigning new recruits once they arrived in France. I suspect that, at the depots to which these men were sent, there would have been a list of regiments with a shortage of men, and that some clerical exercise would have taken place to fill the gaps. In the early days of the war, the policy had been to keep recruits that had joined together from the same location in the same units. The flaw in that initial policy was that whole towns could lose their supply of young men in a single action, as had been tragically demonstrated by the disaster that overtook some of the 'Pals' battalions on the Somme in July 1916.

The *Arcadian* was a Royal Mail steamer that was employed as a troopship and ammunition carrier. She was torpedoed and sunk by a German submarine in the Mediterranean on 15 April 1917; of the 601 troops on board, 75 perished. If Harry had not suffered from bad teeth, obviously requiring attention, at Rugeley, this story might have been very different.

A few days later, Harry wrote to Kate. Things have moved on a little, since his letter to Jack.

13th May, 1917

Dear Kate

Sorry I have not written to you for such a long time no doubt you're being wondering how I am getting on. I should have wrote to you only have been so busy always something to do never any time to spare. I am in the best of health at present the weather here is very hot. We had a good voyage across the channel it was very calm. I think we are going further up the line tomorrow so can't send you my proper address. I shall send it on to Ethel as soon as I get it so you can write for it. I have had some moving about what bit I have been in the army. First I was attached the York's then the South Staffords and West Yorks now I think I am settled in the ninth Batt York & Lancaster so you see I have had some moves. Write as soon as you get my address and let me know how you are getting on. I wrote to Jack and he seems to be getting on alright. I will write again as soon as I can.

With Best Love from

Harry

For whatever reason, at the fourth attempt to find a regiment, Harry joined the 9th (Service) Battalion, the York and Lancaster Regiment, having previously been attached to the Yorkshire Regiment (Green Howards), the South Staffordshire Regiment and the West Yorkshire Regiment.

I can only estimate the date on which he joined the York and Lancasters. Working backwards from his letter to Kate, which is dated, I would guess that the first letter to Jack, when Harry was still with the West Yorkshires, must have been written in the first week in May, which would indicate that he joined the 9th York and Lancasters between the 7th and the 10th.

Referring to the battalion war diary for that month, from 3 to 9 May the 9th was out of the line, undergoing training on the Boescheppe (Boeschepe) training ground, about ten miles (16km) west and slightly south of Ypres, just over the border into France. That would have been a logical time to take in new recruits. On the 10th, the battalion moved to a new camp and on the night of 11th it relieved another unit, taking its place in the front line.

Harry is, at last, 'in the line', in a proper fighting unit, experiencing his first taste of a battlefield on the Western Front. His letter to Kate of 13 May must have been written when he was actually in the front line, for the battalion had been relieved in the trenches by 14 May, and sent by train to Poperinghe (Poperinge), the main British administration and rest centre for the Ypres sector, some six miles (10km) west of the city and well away from the front.

As May progressed, Harry's battalion would be charged with the task of preparing for the major assault on the crucial objective of the Messines Ridge, as a prelude to the coming great offensive, in which the British were to attempt to drive the Germans back from the Ypres Salient. The battalion's role in the coming action would have been determined by now, and the training programme undertaken to ensure that all ranks were properly prepared. It can be said that the imminent battle, unlike so many offensives on the Western Front, generally enjoys a reputation for thorough and meticulous planning and preparation.

CHAPTER 3

FIRST TASTE OF THE TRENCHES

MAY 1917. HARRY IS NOW a trained infantryman, taking his place in the front line, close to the strategically important town of Ypres. What would he have found?

The front line here, as on most of the Western Front, had been virtually static for the last two years. Despite the lack of progress, the level of fighting in this sector had been consistently intense, with enormous losses on both sides. The armies had constructed elaborate defensive positions, vast networks of interlocking trenches with concrete bunkers at strategic points. The trench maps of the time show a mass of fine lines stretching back hundreds of yards from the front line, delineating the first, second and reserve lines of trenches, as well as supply and communication trenches. The map on the jacket of this book shows the German system of trenches near Messines in May 1917, although most of the detail of the British trenches has been omitted for reasons of security.

The forward trenches were defended against infantry attack by deep concentrations of all but impenetrable barbed wire. This wire and the machine guns that covered it made 'no man's land' – the unoccupied area between the opposing trench lines – a killing zone for defenders: lethal for attackers. In any assault, the balance always favoured the defender.

There was, effectively, a deadly stalemate. Generals on both sides were convinced that the war could only be won by decisive attacks, followed by a breakthrough as the enemy crumbled. Neither side had a strategy that could allow these attacks to succeed, or if they did, they did not possess the means – especially reliable tanks, mobile artillery and air superiority – to exploit it.

In the line, Harry would have found well-established, deep trenches with shallow 'funk holes' dug into the sides and underground bunkers as command posts for each company. Food would be carried forward to the men through a network of communication trenches. Hot meals would be brought in 'hay boxes', but were unlikely to be very hot by the time they arrived. Sometimes hot tea could be brewed up on a small stove. Staple rations would be bread (though it would be around eight days old by the time it reached the front), tinned corned beef (bully), jam and maybe 'Maconochie', a kind of tinned stew of meat and vegetables often known, from its manufacturer's name, as 'conner'. There would be the occasional 'treat' arriving in a parcel from home, and Harry celebrated his parcels in his letters. Smoking was encouraged with a substantial tobacco allowance, and, of course, it helped relieve the boredom.

Between major offensives there was daily shelling, patrols and sniper fire, punctuated by the occasional trench raid by either side, localized attacks, usually at night, to achieve a specific purpose, such as to knock out an opposing strongpoint or seize a prisoner to take back and interrogate. As a novice to this kind of warfare, Harry would have been quite vulnerable. Many new arrivals were unable to resist having a quick look at the enemy's trenches,

There are few identifiable photographs of the 9th York and Lancasters during the Great War. This, showing the interior of a typical trench on the Western Front, features men from a another battalion of the same regiment.

(which may have been less than a hundred yards away) only to fall easy prey to a sniper, or a burst of machine-gun fire.

Hygiene was a constant problem. Washing and shaving used up valuable water. It was normal practice to use the last dregs of a mug of tea to shave with one of the new-fangled safety razors that were replacing the 'cut-throat' type. Soldiers just accepted that they were to be filthy and covered in mud for their time in the front line. Heavy infestations of body lice were an inescapable and intolerable fact of trench life, and a dangerous one, for they carry typhus.

The latrine trenches were, astonishingly, often dug in front of the forward trenches, albeit at trench-floor, rather than ground, level. The facility itself would consist of a plank fixed a couple of feet above a hole in the ground. Toilet paper? No chance! – the men used torn-up newspaper or any other 'bumf' (bum fodder) they could lay hands on. The latrines were approached by a communication trench, and were never an inviting prospect. Many soldiers 'improvised'; an empty bully-beef tin, for instance, could be filled and slung over the parapet.

The daily morning 'hate' was part of the routine in the front line. The day almost always started with an exchange of artillery shells, along with rifle and machine-gun fire, beginning just before dawn, the time when an assault was most likely to take place. The 'hate' was a way of discouraging an attack.

Death in the trenches was always a companion. If soldiers 'kept their heads down' they were fairly safe from enemy rifle and machine-gun fire, but shells and mortar bombs were another matter. Gas masks were extremely uncomfortable and made movement or any strenuous activity almost impossible, although they were a reasonably effective protection against the gas. Every front-line trench had gas alarms positioned along it at intervals, usually brass shell cases which, when struck with a metal bar, made a loud bell-like sound. These would be sounded at the first sign of a gas bombardment, causing soldiers to fumble hastily for their masks.

Surviving shelling was a matter of chance. Only the deepest and strongest bunkers could withstand a direct hit, but could act as a sump in which the poison gas would collect. There was no defence against accurate shelling. A shrapnel shell would be packed with ball bearings that scattered when the projectile exploded. If one landed in an occupied section of trench, there would be many casualties. A direct hit from a high-explosive shell would leave little trace of any nearby soldiers. Anyone in the same stretch of trench would certainly be killed or badly wounded. For this reason trenches were not dug in straight lines, but with kinks and corners, often in a geometrical pattern like the battlements of a castle. This also had the merit of preventing any enemy soldiers who might break into a trench from being able to fire along it, since there would be a turn every few yards, screening the next sector.

From time to time small parties of soldiers from either side would venture into no man's land. They would be sent out to repair or strengthen the wire, to reconnoitre the enemy trenches, and perhaps to try to snatch a prisoner for interrogation. Of necessity, these forays would be done under cover of darkness. If the patrols were detected in their work, machine-gun fire could make this a very unpleasant and dangerous occupation.

Even less pleasant were the tasks Harry refers to as 'suicide posts.' These were concealed listening posts in no man's land, often not much more than a shell hole close to the enemy wire, in which a section of men would spend the hours of darkness listening and watching to try to gain some knowledge of the enemy's activities. If they were detected, their chances of surviving were very slim.

By the time Harry arrived, the front line would have stunk of human waste and rotting flesh. It was a smell that the survivors would never forget. In some sections of the line the concentration of death was overwhelming, so that it was almost impossible to extend a trench or dig a latrine without uncovering bodies or parts of bodies.

The ordinary soldier, like Harry, would spend a proportion of his active service in the front line. About a third of his time would be spent there and in the immediate support trenches. A little longer would be spent in reserve, ready to stand to or move in the event of an enemy attack. The rest of the time, about seventy days a year, would be spent in rest areas such as Poperinghe, well behind the line. With a bit of luck, there would also be two weeks' home leave, although Harry, as a newly joined member of his battalion, wouldn't be considered for that for quite some time.

At this point it is worth briefly discussing the basic tactics that were followed by both sides if an attack was to be made. Naturally there were slight variations, but in general this was the pattern that an assault on the Western Front would follow, and which had evolved over nearly three years of warfare.

The enemy trenches would be subjected initially to a heavy artillery bombardment for a long period – it could be several days and nights, and in the case of the Somme offensive lasted for a week. The aim was to 'soften up' the defenders and to destroy barbed-wire entanglements and other obstacles. The men on the receiving end of this would spend their time in as deep shelters as they could find and would be, for the main part, reasonably safe, if uncomfortable, as well as battered by the noise of the barrage. In general, however, the effect of the bombardment on wire entanglements was minimal. The shells, high-explosive or shrapnel, would just redistribute the wire slightly without cutting it, adding shell holes to the other obstructions that the attackers needed to overcome.

On the morning of the attack, almost always just before dawn, the shelling would stop and the first line of attacking troops, fortified with a rum ration, would go 'over the top', leaving the safety of their trenches to advance across no man's land.

Since the routine was accepted as standard procedure by both sides, there were no surprises. As soon as the bombardment stopped or shifted, the defenders would man the firing steps, ready with machine guns and rifles to repel the enemy, while their own artillery fired in support

By 1917, the role of the artillery supporting an attack had changed. Since the Somme, instead of bombarding the enemy's support trenches and rear areas once an assault had started, they were now required to provide a 'creeping barrage', in which fire would be aimed to land in no man's land just ahead of the advancing troops. As the attacking infantry moved forward the point of impact would be raised to maintain the same distance ahead of them. The smoke and debris would hide the advance and make it more difficult for the defenders to counter it. In theory . . .

In practice, it was not as simple as the theory suggested. The shelling had to be accurate. The shells were not, at that time, consistently made and a proportion would drop short and land among the attackers; the same could happen if a gun's barrel was worn. The barrage had to be synchronized in time and space with the attack. Only the start time was manageable. From then on, the plan was to advance the barrage at a fixed rate of 100 yards per minute. The infantry had to stick to that or their assault would go badly wrong: if they advanced too quickly they would walk into the 'friendly fire'; too slowly, and the barrage would get too far ahead, giving the defenders, warned of the attack by that barrage, time to man their defensive positions and use rifle and machine gun to good effect – doubly terrifying and deadly if the attack were to be held up by the barbed wire.

Of course, communication was almost impossible. There was no practical portable radio, and field-telephone lines, unreeled behind the advance, were easily damaged by shelling. This left 'runners', individual soldiers sent back with important information or requests for support, reinforcements or supplies, or forward with orders, changes to plan, and so on. Needless to say, casualties among runners were severe. In addition, the smoke and dust in the half light of the dawn made signalling or observation a real challenge. In the light of all this, plans had to be carefully made and stuck to, to the letter, if there was to be any chance of success.

This was the world that Harry entered in May 1917. Experiencing the front line for the first time, he had to learn to cope with the horrific conditions. There was no alternative. For the first time, he writes to both Jack and Kate after seeing and experiencing at first hand the horror of the front line. The two letters were written on the same day, but each has a slightly different emphasis.

June 2/6/1917

   Dear Jack
*Very pleased to receive a letter from you and to hear you are going on
all right. We have had a very rough time lately the Germans were only
about 40yds away from us, we had a very trying time for the first, but
I don't care so long that I keep alright. It will be a good job when the
war is over. Ethel tells me they are alright at home but Willie as got a
cough. Hope will soon be better. I hear Connie has started school and
that she likes it. I hope that she gets on alright. I have not received a
letter from Kate yet but expect one any time. this is my address 32507
9th Batt York and Lancs, C Company, 11 platoon in B.E.F* [British
Expeditionary Force; he later transferred to 12 Platoon] *France.
I think I am going in for a Lewis Gunner. I don't know yet I will let
you know next time I write we are having a bit of a practice this last
day or two we have been out of the trenches. We get plenty of tobacco
but little bread out here. Write to me when you receive this letter and
let me know all you can. I am glad to receive a letter.*
   With Best Love from
   Harry

Harry doesn't sound too impressed with his new environment.
After a few days he's very keen for the war to be over. The German
front-line trench seems to be incredibly close, less than the width
of a football pitch. Since a standard-issue rifle in the hands of a
modestly competent marksman can easily pick off a man at 200
yards, this is not a situation for the faint-hearted!

The Lewis gun was the standard light machine gun used by
the British infantry. It was an air-cooled, gas-operated weapon
equipped with a circular drum magazine on top of the barrel,
usually holding forty-seven rounds of 0.303-inch ammunition
– the same round as that used in the standard-issue rifle, the
famous Short Magazine Lee-Enfield. Each platoon would have a
machine-gun section with one Lewis gunner, the 'number one',
who aimed and fired the weapon, a 'number two' who handled
the replacement of magazines and assisted if the weapon jammed,
and seven others to give covering rifle fire and to carry spare

Part of a Lewis-gun section of the York and Lancaster Regiment (although not the 9th Battalion). The number one is cleaning the receiver ready to accept the magazine; in the background, the number two is loading rounds into one of the circular drum magazines.

The principle parts of the Lewis light machine gun, from a contemporary encyclopedia. Harry spent all his active service as a member of a Lewis-gun section. In one of his letters, Harry asks Jack to send him 'a small book on the Lewis Gun'.

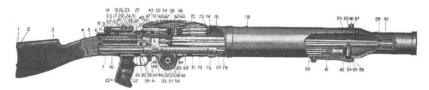

LEWIS AUTOMATIC LIGHT MAGAZINE GUN

1, Butt plate; 2, butt plate screws; 3, butt; 4, butt tang screw; 5, butt tang; 6, feed cover latch; 7, butt latch, securing butt to receiver; 8, back sight bed spring; 9, back sight bed spring screw; 10, butt latch spring; 11, back sight bed; 12, feed cover latch pin; 13, feed cover; 14, back sight leaf; 15, back sight thumb piece; 16, back sight slide catch; 17, back sight fine adj. worm; 18, back sight fine adj. worm axis pin; 19, back sight slide catch spring; 20, back sight slide; 22, Firing hand grip; 22A, guard side rivets; 23, back sight axis pin washer; 24, back sight axis pin; 25, back sight axis washer fixing pin; 26, receiver; 27, magazine pawls spring; 30, trigger; 31, feed operating stud; 33, trigger pin; 34, feed operating arm; 37, bolt that closes breech and takes shock of discharge; 39, guard; 40, cartridge guide spring; 41, sear spring; 42, sear; 43, magazine pan; 46, gear stop; 47, striker fixing pin; 48, gear stop pin; 49, gear stop spring; 50, striker; 51, cartridge spacer; 52, gear operated by main spring; 53, main spring casing; 54 magazine top plate rivets; 55, main spring which closes breech and returns parts to firing position; 56, collet pin; 57, main spring collet; 58, magazine centre; 59, main spring rivets; 60, magazine latch spring; 61, gear casing; 62, magazine latch; 64, gear casing side piece; 65, gear case hinge pin; 66, feed operating arm latch; 67, magazine top plate; 68, receiver lock pin; 69, cartridge spacer rivets; 70, interior cartridge separators; 71, radiator casing rear, locking piece; 72, rack, actuated by piston and main spring; 73, Radiator casing rear, platform; 74, radiator casing rear; 75, piston connecting pin; 76, barrel; 77, gas cylinder; 78, radiator for cooling barrel; 79, piston operated by gases of exploding cartridge that ejects empty shell and resets firing pin; 80, regulator key stud; 81, gas regulator key; 82, gas chamber; 83, gas port; 84, gas regulator; 85, clamp ring; 86, fore sight; 87, clamp ring positioning screw; 88, clamp ring screw; 89, barrel mouth piece; 90, radiator casing front.

magazines. Each member of the section would carry, in addition to his kit and his own rifle and ammunition, eight charged Lewis magazines, each weighing 4.5 pounds (2kg). All members of the section were trained to take over if the number one or two became a casualty. And, of course, a Lewis gun in action would rapidly become a priority target for the enemy's fire. From his letter to Jack, however, it sounds as though Harry volunteered for this special role.

Harry's letter to Kate on the same day makes no mention of the Lewis-gun section, nor of anything else that might have been considered dangerous.

2nd June 1917

> *Dear Kate,*
>
> *I received your letter. I am pleased to hear you are going on alright they all seem to be getting on all right at home which is something to be thankful for. The weather here is lovely and we have had a fine time this last fortnight. We are still out of the trenches but we might go back anytime. Jack has wrote me telling me he has had to leave his lodging and go to the vicarage – I hope he gets on all right. Write soon and let me know how you are getting on. Jack has sent me some sardines and chicken paste which is all right here and it works the bread and butter down. I am glad Connie is going on alright at school I don't think it will do her any harm. They tell me Willie and Connie keep very good friends which I am glad to hear.*
>
> *With best love from*
> *Harry*

Note the difference between what he tells his brother and what he writes to Kate. 'We have had a very rough time lately,' as against 'we have had a fine time this last fortnight'.

Here we also have Harry's first mention of the food at the front. It has been estimated that the soldiers' bread would have taken a full eight days between baking and reaching the front line; no surprise, then, that it took some 'working down.' I think, too, that Harry is saying that the extra victuals from home are

With love to
Connie from Harry
x x x x x

Modèle déposé A. O. — Visé, Paris

Dear Connie
I hope you are
a good girl and
keep friends with
Willie how do
you like school
With love
from Harry

An embroidered
card Harry sent to
Connie after she
had started school.

welcome. Perhaps, very politely, he is also hoping to prompt
another package, this time from sister Kate.

Connie, who is seven years old by this time, is at school. That
must be a milestone. With the cerebral palsy, and the resulting
difficulty in walking, it would have been a major achievement.
From Mill Street in Ilkeston she would probably have gone to
Chaucer Street School, as did Willie once he was old enough.
Coincidentally, Willie's wife, Nancy (my mother), was to teach
there many years later.

By the first week in June Harry has been with C Company, 9th
Battalion, York and Lancaster Regiment, for around three weeks.
From the battalion's war diary we can work out that he spent
three or four days in the front line and a similar time in support.
He would have experienced shelling and a gas attack, both of
which caused casualties. Significantly, he would have repeatedly
practised the routine for an assault on the training-ground area at
Boescheppe, behind the lines, which had been set up using flags
to mimic the enemy's positions on a part of the Messines Ridge,
a small rise in the ground known as Mount Sorrel.

A British trench map from 1917, showing a part of the Ypres Salient, with German trenches and wire entanglements marked.

By then, he had seen what shelling could do, as the war diary for 12 May records: 'D's Company Headquarters dugout had been blown in about 5.30 a.m. 2Lt [Second Lieutenant] Bunce S.H. was wounded & 2Lt Proctor M. & 2Lt Breingen S.K. were killed.' (The war diary only records the names of officers; casualties among other ranks are recorded just by their number.) Following that, when in the reserve line, a 5.9-inch shell blew in the battalion orderly room and 'records and papers were destroyed'. Any men hurt? Nothing is recorded.

The war diary goes on to log the total casualties for that tour in the front line: 'Officers 1 wounded, 2 killed. O.R. [other ranks] 4 killed, 24 wounded.' This was rather different from working in a lace factory.

Also noted is the fact that for five days of that month, May, 'The Bn [battalion] practised offensive for MT SORREL system on a flag course situated in the BOESCHEPE training area.' From this and other indicators, the men of the 9th York and Lancasters would have known that they were to be involved in serious warfare in the very near future. Harry would be going 'over the top' for the first time. That prospect must have been chilling.

CHAPTER 4

MESSINES RIDGE

THE FIRST WEEK OF JUNE 1917 was a significant one on the
Flanders battlefields.

The Messines–Wytschaete (Mesen–Wijtschate) Ridge is nothing
particularly special on the ground. Visit it today and there is
simply a slightly higher area, largely covered in trees, which
extends from Messines in the south, to Zillebeke in the north.

Some of the names given to the hills during the campaign
there illustrate the reality of the 'high' ground west and south-
west of Ypres. 'Hill 60' and 'Hill 62' rise 60 metres and 62
metres (66 and 68 yards) above sea level respectively. The
plain stretching towards Ypres, then occupied by the Allies,
lies at between 50 and 55 metres (55 and 60 yards) above sea

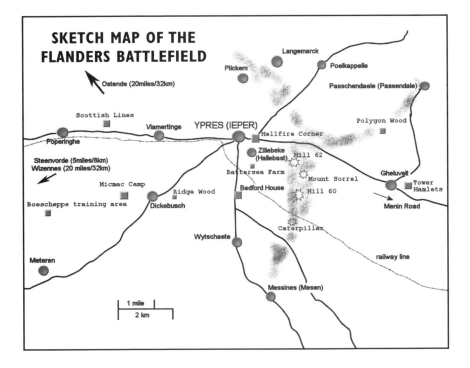

SKETCH MAP OF THE
FLANDERS BATTLEFIELD

Ostende (20miles/32km)

Langemarck

Pilckem

Poelkappelle

Passchendaele (Passendale)

Scottish Lines

Vlamertinge

YPRES (IEPER)

Polygon Wood

Poperinghe

Hellfire Corner

Steenvorde (5miles/8km)
Wizennes (20 miles/32km)

Zillebeke
(Hallebast)

Hill 62

Battersea Farm

Micmac Camp

Ridge Wood

Mount Sorrel

Ghekuvelt

Bedford House

Hill 60

Tower
Hamlets

Boescheppe training area

Dickebusch

Menin Road

Meteren

Wytschaete

Caterpillar

railway line

Messines (Mesen)

1 mile

2 km

level. The flatness of the Flanders landscape means, however, that even the smallest rise dominates the surrounding country.

In 1917, the German Army occupied the whole ridge, forming a minor salient into the Allies' territories. It became an important objective for the next offensive. Field Marshal Sir Douglas Haig, Commander-in-Chief of the British armies on the Western Front, gave the task of taking the ridge to General Sir Herbert Plumer, commanding the Second Army in the Ypres Salient. His planning and preparation, which lasted for months (hence the model of the ridge used for training during Harry's time at Rugeley), were meticulous. The most significant element was the siting of huge explosive mines deep underneath the German positions. Sappers (Royal Engineers), for once given a job true to their title, became tunnellers. (The word 'sapper' derives from the tunnels and other earthworks which, in earlier centuries, were dug under fortifications to 'sap' their strength during a siege.) Men who were miners in civilian life were drafted in to dig tunnels under no man's land to reach a point beneath the German front line on the ridge. The whole undertaking spanned more than a year, but on completion the sappers had planted a total of almost five hundred tons of high explosive in twenty-one mines across the six miles or so of the ridge.

The tunnelling was hazardous. There was always the possibility of collapse. Moreover, the Germans knew that the British were working underground, with the result that both sides were tunnelling and counter-tunnelling at the same time and each maintained listening posts, trying to detect the enemy's activities. There were occasions when one side would break into the other's tunnel, and in the darkness hand-to-hand fighting would often follow.

Eventually, by the end of May, all was in place on the ground, ready for the assault. The troops had been carefully trained. As we have seen, Harry's battalion spent five days practising on the Boescheppe training ground where their objective, Mount Sorrel, had been simulated with an arrangement of flags. Harry would already have gained an overview of the whole ridge from the mock-up at the Cannock Chase training area before he even crossed the Channel.

General Plumer (later Field Marshal Viscount Plumer of Messines) – his intelligence, detailed planning and care for his men belied his almost comical looks. (From a painting after a portrait by William Orpen.)

The orders for the operation would have been passed down from General Plumer, via his staff, to the different levels of command. On receipt of these, Lieutenant-Colonel Bowes-Wilson, commanding the 9th York and Lancasters, prepared written orders for his officers. (These may be seen at the National Archives at Kew, as may the battalion war diary.)

Responsibility for the operation was, for once in that war, in the correct hands. General Plumer, a skilful commander who did everything he could in the circumstances to minimize casualties among his soldiers, and who was in consequence liked and admired by them, appreciated the problems that his troops would encounter and made sure that they were dealt with as effectively as possible. He learned from the use of mines in the initial British assault at the Battle of the Somme, almost a year earlier. On that occasion, there had been a ten-minute pause between the firing of the explosive charges and the signal to attack. That gave the defenders time to recover their composure, man their positions and take control of no man's land. At Messines, by contrast, there was to be only a minute's gap between the blast and the start of the assault.

During the first few days of June, Harry's battalion moved towards the launch point for the coming offensive. Still they were vulnerable, as the war diary records: 'There were two casualties on the way to camp owing to enemy shelling back areas with gas shells.' Then, 'On the evening of 6th Bn moved to assembly positions previous to the attack.' The diary adds, 'There were no casualties whilst the Bn was assembling.'

For ten days and ten nights up to 6 June 1917, the lives of Harry and the other members of C Company had been dominated by the sight and sounds of the continuous artillery bombardment of the German defensive positions (approximately 1 shell every 2 seconds, incessantly for 240 hours).

By now, the eve of the attack, the battalion was in the line, waiting in the forward trenches for the order to advance across no man's land on to the German trenches. Each soldier had with him his full battle kit, steel helmet, personal weapon, respirator, food, water, ammunition – everything he would need had to be carried. Harry, as a member of 12 Platoon's Machine-Gun Section, would also be carrying extra magazines for the Lewis gun, greatly increasing the total load he would have to take into action. We can see from the squad photograph taken at Rugeley that he was not a large man. (A full list of what the attacking troops from the 9th York and Lancasters had to carry is given on pages 50–1.)

The forward trenches were deep, with a firing step on the side facing the enemy. Dug into the trench walls were small bolt holes, which were all the soldiers had for shelter from the elements and the enemy's shelling. Sleep would have been impossible. The bombardment was intense and continuous. The soldiers would have hoped that it would do its job in softening up, or even destroying, the German defences. Veterans of the Somme, the previous year, would have known that this was a vain hope. Both the 9th York and Lancasters and its sister battalion in 70 Brigade, the 8th, had been heavily involved on the first day of that battle, suffering appalling casualties.

Harry had been in Flanders for only three weeks. During that time he had already spent three days in the front line, followed by four days in immediate reserve. He was now about to go into action for the first time.

There is no doubt that by now everyone would have known perfectly well what was about to happen. A combination of training exercises and rumour would have alerted the ordinary infantryman to the fact that a big 'push' was in the offing, while the commencement of the artillery bombardment days earlier would have confirmed that it was imminent. Many were just anxious to 'get it over with' – however horrifically it might eventually turn out. The Germans in that sector would also have been well aware of imminent action. The continuous bombardment sent a message that an attack was a certainty.

As it happened, during the night of the 6/7 June, the German front-line troops in the defensive positions on the Messines Ridge were relieved. The replacement body of troops moved in and once they were in position the relieved unit would move out, back to the reserve areas. At 3.10 a.m. on 7 June, however, both sets of troops were in the German positions.

In the sector of the British line occupied by Harry's company, the cry was 'No bloody rum!' For the British troops, there was always an issue of rum before they went over the top. In the chilly pre-dawn, a good swig of rum helped with the chill as well as the courage. Perhaps it got lost on its way up the line, or maybe their big earthenware carboy was broken. For whatever reason, C Company missed out on its rum ration that day.

At 2.50 a.m., still dark, the order came that the troops were to lie down. Of course, this would have been rehearsed, occasioning rumours and speculation among the men, but not many would have known the real reason for the 'lying-down drill'.

At 3.10 a.m. precisely, nineteen mines, totalling 450 tons of high explosive, were electrically detonated beneath the German

A page from the written orders issued by Lieutenant-Colonel Bowes-Wilson, CO of the 9th York and Lancasters, for the attack on the Messines Ridge on 7 June 1917. Like many of his men, Colonel Bowes-Wilson did not survive the day.

positions on the Messines–Wytschaete Ridge. The biggest ever man-made explosion to date ripped the top from the ridge, killing or entombing thousands of German soldiers.

Well over a year in preparation, of the twenty-one mines laid only nineteen detonated that morning. One had been discovered and neutralized by the Germans, and the other either failed to detonate or was not needed on the day, and in time their whereabouts was forgotten. (On 17 July 1955 a lightning strike set off one of the missing mines. The only casualty: a cow, and an aggrieved Belgian farmer suddenly confronted with a new, massive, crater on his land. The twenty-first mine, the one the Germans discovered, is said to have been found, but not removed.)

The British had used remotely fired mines on the Western Front before, and so the strategy was understood, but they had certainly never used them on this scale. In his briefing to his general staff before the battle, Plumer had remarked: 'Gentlemen, we may not make history tomorrow, but we shall certainly change the geography.' In fact, they did both.

The explosion was incredible. One eyewitness, the war correspondent Philip Gibbs, writing in the *Morning Chronicle*, described the massive detonation:

> *The most diabolical splendour I have ever seen. Out of the dark ridges of Messines and Wytschaete and the ill-famed Hill 60, there gushed out and up enormous volumes of scarlet flame from the exploding mines and of earth and smoke all lighted by the flame spilling over into mountains of fierce colour, so that all the countryside was illuminated with red light. While some of us stood watching, aghast and spellbound by this burning horror, the ground trembled and surged violently to and fro. Truly the earth quaked . . .*

What must it have been like for the assault troops in the front line? Would part of the lying-down drill have included ordering the soldiers to cover their ears? Harry makes no mention of the blast in his letters. Perhaps he was deafened by the preceding bombardment. Maybe the troops had been ordered not to mention it in letters.

Maybe he just didn't find it that astonishing; after all, he hadn't been at the front long enough to establish what was 'normal'.

A map of British dispositions for the attack shows that Harry's company was in trenches around two hundred yards from two of the underground mines. One has to wonder whether many of the troops were deafened, although by now they were well used to the sound of the artillery barrage. Yet this was something unprecedented – the noise of the combined explosions was so great that in England the Prime Minister, David Lloyd George, forewarned of the time of the attack, had himself woken at his Surrey home ten minutes before zero hour so that he could listen for the blast. Official sources confirm that Lloyd George did indeed hear the distant rumble of sound, and even felt the tremors of the shock wave. The newspapers reported that people in the south-east of England were woken by it; some reports even claimed that the shock wave travelled as far as Dublin. That Harry does not mention hearing it means nothing, however. He wasn't a man for detail – or for causing unnecessary anxiety among his people at home.

Almost immediately after the explosion, officers blew their whistles and the front-line troops left their trenches and started to advance towards the German positions. Harry's company was the third wave over, following on 200 yards behind the first wave of men, and tasked with supporting the main attack.

The equipment list for each soldier, set out in the orders for the battalion, brings home the challenge that faced these men as the whistles sounded, even before they came under enemy fire:

All Officers will be dressed and equipped the same as the men; sticks are not to be carried [this was to prevent the enemy identifying officers and directing snipers to fire on them].

Fighting Order for all ranks:-
(a) Clothing, Arms and Entrenching Tool, as issued.
(b) Equipment as issued with the exception of the pack. Haversacks are to be worn on the back, except for Lewis Gunners, Rifle Bombers and carrying parties, who will wear it at the side.

(c) Box Respirators and P.H. Helmets ['small box respirator' or 'SBR' and 'phenate hexamine helmet', types of gas mask].

(d) Iron Rations, unexpended portion of the day's rations, Mess tin and cover.

(e) 120 rounds S.A.A. [small-arms ammunition] *except Bombers, Signallers, Runners, Lewis Gunners and Rifle Bombers who carry 50 rounds. Carrying Parties, 50 rounds S.A.A.*

(f) Every man (except bombing sections) two Mills Bombs [hand grenades] *one in each top pocket. These Bombs will be collected into dumps as soon as the Objective has been gained.*

(g) Moppers Up and Carrying Parties will not carry flares, nor will carrying parties carry (f).

(h) Three sandbags per man for Moppers Up only.

(i) Water Bottle, full.

(j) Mopping Up parties will carry one 'P' Bomb [phosphorus grenade; i.e. a smoke bomb] *in addition to two Mills Bombs.*

(k) Bombing Sections will carry:-

(1) Bayonet Men 6 Mills Bombs.

(2) Remainder of Section, 12 Mills Bombs per man.

(l) Bombing Sections of Mopping Up Parties will carry 10 Mills Bombs and 1 'P' Bomb per man.

The concession in (h) for Lewis gunners like Harry was to enable them to carry an extra eight magazines. Since the equipment he would have to take into action would weigh more than 65 pounds (30kg), the extra magazines meant that his load would be in excess of 100 pounds (45kg). Any personal 'extras' would also need to be carried.

The entry in the battalion war diary for that day explains:

At 0310 (zero hour) our artillery opened up a terrific barrage on the Hun front line & simultaneously the mines under Hill 60 and the Caterpillar were blown. At zero + 1 [minute] *the first wave consisting of B Coy on the left & A Coy on the right went over, and were followed by D Coy (moppers up) & C Coy* [Harry's] *in support at short intervals.*

That there was initially little opposition to the assault is unsurprising. Estimates suggest that around ten thousand German defenders died instantly in the explosion. Some were vaporized, others had their internal organs destroyed by the shock wave from the blast, others still were buried beneath tons of dirt and debris. With a front of around six miles (10km), that works out, roughly, at the equivalent of an entire British battalion wiped out for each 1,000 yards (900 metres) of front line, or a man for every yard. Understandably, the badly shaken and demoralized survivors offered little resistance. In the case of the German troops in the positions assaulted by the 9th York and Lancasters, their casualties must have been virtually doubled because both the outgoing unit and the replacement troops were in the line when the mines blew.

There was some ineffective resistance from a few Germans in pockets along the line, but the attack was only held up briefly. Large numbers of the enemy, dazed and disoriented, surrendered without a fight; others, uninjured, also held up their hands, happy to get away from this hellhole of the war. In all, 5,000 German prisoners were taken. Many of them laughed with relief and shook hands with the Tommies who had overrun their shattered positions.

For all their success against the German infantry, the mines would have had little impact on the German artillery positions sited well behind the front lines. As soon as the assault began the defenders' guns would have been directed on to the attacking troops.

Harry's battalion attacked behind a creeping artillery barrage from the British guns. As we have seen, the shells should have fallen in front of them as they advanced. But it was not an exact science, and many British casualties were caused by 'friendly fire'.

The 9th York and Lancasters had been assigned the part of the ridge that contained Hill 60 as well as Mount Sorrel. A and D Companies were in the first two waves. Harry's C Company waited in a newly dug trench behind the front line.

The battalion's orders for the day are precise and chilling. In them, Lieutenant-Colonel Bowes-Wilson – who was to be killed at noon that day – writes:

At Zero, Mines under HILL 60 & the CATERPILLAR will be fired.
18-pounders [the standard British field gun] *will barrage the enemy front line.*
Zero + 1 [minute] *Barrage lifts & will move slowly back allowing for a pace of 25 yards a minute.*
Zero + 20 Barrage lifts off battalion objective & will pause about 200 yards in front of this line till zero plus 3 hours 40 minutes.
Zero + 3 hours. Barrage again lifts & allows C & D 40 minutes. Bns to advance to take their objective.

The CO goes on to describe how the three waves (Harry in the third, not the fifth as he says in a letter he sent after the action) are to cross no man's land at 100-yard intervals. The positions of the medical officers and dressing stations are indicated, as is the route back for stretcher cases and walking wounded.

Harry's company is to support the first wave:

If necessary, the O.C. [officer commanding] *'C' Company must push on to the Bn objective to help A & B Companies gain this.*

Immediately the Bn objective has been gained, a line in, or in front of this, must be consolidated. Lines must be firestepped & organized to resist counter attacks. Wiring to be commenced as soon as possible.

All very clear. All very clinical. Of course, the firesteps in the German trenches would be facing the wrong way for defence against any counter-attack from the enemy's rear, and the wire would be behind what would have become the front line if the battalion took its objectives.

How did the assault go? The answer is, very well at first. As the war diary records:

The attack progressed very favourably and by zero + 30 the Bn had reached its objective and began consolidating. Very few casualties were sustained in the actual attack.

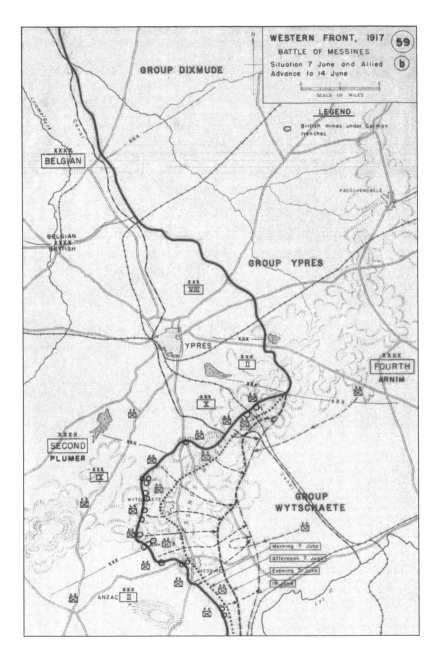

A map showing the positions of the mines beneath the Messines–Wytschaete Ridge, and the subsequent British gains.

The remains of a German strongpoint on Mount Sorrel, the battalion's objective on the Messines Ridge, after the detonation of the mines.

So far, so good. The 9th York and Lancasters had reached Mount Sorrel and occupied the enemy's front-line positions there with few casualties.

The obvious strategy of carrying on with the advance beyond the first objective was not considered. The objective had been to take the high ground at the Messines Ridge and then to set up defensive positions there.

The German Army would have been alarmed, if not dismayed, by its losses on that morning, and so rapidly responded with intense artillery fire. As the British troops had taken over the German trenches, their positions were known precisely and the German artillery had little problem in finding the mark. The war diary, 9 June 1917, two days after the initial assault:

The Bn remained in its objectives until the evening of the 9th. During this period the Bn underwent heavy shelling & sustained many casualties. B Coy also relieved the 8th Bn Y & L in the front line on the morning of the 9th. On the evening of the 9th the Bn was relieved by the 1st N Staffs [North Staffordshire Regiment] Bn. The total casualties sustained were officers – killed 4 (including the C.O.) wounded 6. O.R.s – Killed 39, wounded 211. Died of wounds 9. Missing 18.

The casualties represent well over a quarter of the battalion. Almost 10 per cent had been killed or were missing. (Most of the 'missing' were likely to have been killed by shelling, buried by the action or simply blown to pieces.) The proportion of killed to wounded was smaller than would have been expected from an assault against machine guns. At the Somme, in some battalions twice as many men were killed as were wounded. This confirms that the casualties largely came from the shelling once the objective had been reached.

> *Night of 9th/10th. On relief the Bn moved by motor lorry from KRUISTRAAT to SCOTTISH LINES. Capt. D Lewis took over temp command of Bn at midday on June 7th (from Lt Col Bowes-Wilson, killed in action 7.6.17*). Coys at O.C. Coys* [i.e. companies to be at their company commanders'] *disposal for cleaning up and re-organization.* [*Added in very small writing as a superscript.]

With a new temporary battalion commander (a captain taking a lieutenant-colonel's job shows the extent of the casualties), on 10 June the battalion moved away from the front lines to the relatively safe location of Scottish Lines. There were several rest locations for the troops around Poperinghe (Poperinge), about five miles (8km) due west of Ypres. They would have been accommodated in wooden huts – very similar to the ones in the training camp at Rugeley – and much, much more comfortable than the trenches. There, Harry wrote letters to Jack and to Kate, taking care, because of the censorship of the men's letters, not to mention specific place names.

June 11th /1917

> Dear Jack
>
> *I was very pleased to hear from you and that you are going on all right I have been to the place you mentioned in your letter we went there for our bath about a fortnight ago. The part of the line that we are in is straight forward so you will know where I am. We have had another terrible time this week the men here say it was worst than the Somme advance last July. We lost a lot of men but we got where we were asked to take. It was awful*

I am alright got buried and knocked about but quite well now and hope to remain so. We were praised by the general and all, everybody said we had done well, quite a success. I will tell you more when I see you. Mention the name of the place you think I am in and I will tell you whether you are right but I think you will know one of the worst fronts on the line but I think we are having a change of place. When you receive this letter write back and let me know all news you can. It is a rum job waiting for the time to come to go over the top without any rum too. The C.O. got killed and our captain, marvellous how we escaped. The biggest part of our company are scotch man from the Scottish Borderers. I can't tell what they say they are not like Yorkshire men and we were the fifth wave over. I am glad they are alright at home and getting on well. The little book you sent is very nice it will come in useful I will read it. Glad you have wrote to Kate. My address is the same Y & L. I will write again And soon and let you know how I am getting on.

    With best love from

    Harry

(PS) could you send me a small tin of salts or lemon something to put to water only a small tin, anything that will not take up much room.

'I am alright got buried and knocked about' – Harry is probably describing his experience when a shell landed close to him. The earth would have been thrown up to bury him, and he would certainly have felt the blast. Clearly, he had been doubly fortunate, for he was missed by the shrapnel and was able to escape from the burial.

The 'worst than the Somme advance last July' reference is curious, for Harry was plainly misinformed. The Somme had been a disaster for the 9th Battalion, York and Lancaster Regiment. Second in line to go over the top on the infamous first day of the battle (after their sister battalion, the 8th, which suffered even higher casualties), the battalion was cut to pieces by German machine-gun fire. One report claims that it suffered 432 all ranks killed on the morning of 1 July 1916, with total casualties, killed, wounded and missing, of almost 80 per cent of the committed battalion strength of 25 officers and 736 other ranks (a further 10 per cent of every infantry unit involved were kept back from any major assault). Surely the survivors of that massacre would not compare it with the recent action at Messines?

Harry's reference to 'scotch' men in the battalion also has its origins in the Somme battle. After such heavy casualties, replacements were urgently needed. Some severely depleted battalions were disbanded and their troops moved to other units to make up their strength. As part of that exercise, fifty-seven men of the King's Own Scottish Borderers joined the battalion; it may be that, quite sensibly, they were kept together in C Company.

As usual, Harry's letter to Kate spares her some of the more alarming details that he had told Jack:

June 11th /1917

Dear Kate

I was very pleased to receive your packet everything came in very useful. I was very pleased to hear you are going on all right did you receive my letter. We have had some very rough times up here lately especially the last time we were in the trenches you see we had to go over the top. its a rotten time waiting for the order. we had to go over at three in the morning. the bombardment was awful [I was] lucky to get out but I'm very pleased to say I am alright and hope to remain so. There was a parcel waiting for me from Ethel and Annie when I came out, it was nice to have some cake and tea. we never had anything but water for about a week, biscuits and bully a bit of Jam but never mind I got over it. I am very pleased Connie is going to school I do hope she gets on alright – I think they all keep well at home. The weather here is very hot I wish it was a bit cooler. Do not be long before you write. My address is 32507 [his regimental number] ninth York and Lancs Batt C Company L. G. [Lewis gun] section B.E.F. France. There is nobody in my company from our way not that I know of you see a mix them up now there is a lot of scotch men with us you can hardly tell what they say. I have been a with the Lewis gunners the last month but I don't know for how long. It was only three of us came back out of our section after the last fight. I think this is all just now, I will write again soon and tell you more.

With love from

Harry

On Active Service

Received 21. 6. 17

Y.M.C.A.

**WITH THE BRITISH
EXPEDITIONARY FORCE**

Y.M.C.A.

Dear Kate

I was very pleased to receive your packett everything came in very useful. I was very pleased to hear you are going on alright did you receive my letter. We have had some very rough times up here lately especially last time we were in the trenches, you see we had to go over the top, its a rotten time waiting for the order, we had to go over at three in the morning, the bombardment was awful lucky to get out, but I am very pleased to say I am alright and hope to remain so. There was a parcel waiting for me, from Ethel & Annie when I came out, it was nice to have some cake and tea we never had anything but water for about a week, biscuits and bully a bit of jam, but never mind I got over it I am very pleased Connie is going to school I do hope she gets on alright, I think they all keep well a home. The weather here is very hot I wish it was a bit cooler. It not be long before you write. My address 32 507. 9th York + Lancs, Batt. C, Company B.E.F. France. There is nobody in my L.G. Section, company from our way not that

The YMCA provided facilities for troops,
including writing paper, in its establishments
behind the British lines.

'Only three came back out of our section.' A Lewis-gun section would have had nine members at full strength. Harry was a lucky man.

Altogether, the German death toll in the Messines Ridge battle was 25,000, the Allies' 17,000. This time, at least, Harry wasn't among the casualties. The battle was also a very rare example in that war of a successful major assault in which the defenders suffered higher casualties than the attackers, Much of the credit for that belongs to Plumer, who had begun his military career as an officer of the York and Lancaster Regiment; his infantry training, in a war in which so many senior British commanders were cavalrymen, gave him considerable understanding of the ordinary foot soldier. The troops under his command appreciated his meticulous planning and his concern for their welfare, especially in seeking to minimize casualties among them, and nicknamed him 'Daddy' or 'Old Plum'; at his funeral in 1932 some 30,000 of his former soldiers stood in the rain to honour him.

As a contrast, to end the chapter we have a letter from Jack the clergyman in Hull, to Kate, the midwife in Leeds, written on the day of the Battle of Messines, but naturally oblivious to the carnage in Flanders. This is the only letter that has turned up to complete the loop of correspondents.

20 Ryde St, Hull, 7th June 1917

Dear Kate
Just a line to let you know that I've heard from Harry this morning. He would very much like to hear from you. His address is
    Pte H. Lamin
    32507
    9th Batt
    York & Lancashire [sic] Regiment
    C Company
    12th Platoon
    B.E.F. France
He is in very good health I am thankful to say.

I hope you will get on all right with your exam. Have you seen the question papers of former years and do you know off by heart the act of parliament you ought to. I see you had another air raid not very far from London. Did you hear anything of it? I am in the best of health although very hard worked. Mr Thomas [probably a neighbour, but sadly now untraceable] *is very interested in his work in France.*

With lots of love

J. E. Lamin

Note the salutation and ending, which are very formal for a brother writing to his younger sister, even in those days, and even allowing for the seven-year difference in their ages. As to Kate's reward for success in the examination, she passed with flying colours and received a wonderful vellum certificate and a glorious-sounding job title.

CHAPTER 5

THE SUMMER OF 1917

HARRY HAS CLEARED A MAJOR hurdle, surviving the Battle of Messines more or less unscathed. That action was deemed successful, but among many other casualties had resulted in the loss of his battalion commander, his company commander and six out of nine of his own section. The defenders, unusually for a major attack on the Western Front, lost more troops than the attackers, the balance tipped by the 10,000 Germans estimated to have died when the mines were set off. Most of the Allies' losses occurred after the 'successful' initial assault. Nevertheless, the enemy had been driven from the ridge, and the southern end of the Ypres Salient had been secured for the next major Allied attack, due to kick off in July.

Harry, after a month or so in Flanders, will be beginning to understand the reality of trench warfare and will have acquired the essential survival techniques. He will be learning to deal with the severe environment of the front line. He has experienced the intense fear that comes with 'going over the top' (without any rum, too). In short, he is becoming a battle-hardened soldier.

An animated map of the front line close to Ypres for the two years from June 1915 would have shown it wriggling backwards and forwards a few hundred yards this way and that, but, overall, hardly moving at all. By the summer of 1917, however, the whole area would be devastated by the shelling and by the operations of war: trench works, strongpoints, supply roads, gun lines, ammunition dumps, fuel depots, and so on. An enormous proportion of the dead would simply be left where they fell, to be buried by shell blast or exhumed by the same process. There would be no great incentive to risk life and limb to recover the body of someone who was beyond help. On the Menin Gate Memorial at Ypres are the names of nearly 55,000 British, Dominion and Imperial soldiers whose final resting place is unknown. The memorial arbitrarily records only those killed up to mid-August

1917; a further 34,984 names are recorded on the Memorial to the Missing at Tyne Cot cemetery near Passchendaele, and many soldiers from New Zealand and Newfoundland are honoured on separate memorials. These monuments show the scale of the losses at Ypres. The traumatic effect of all this on a conscript from a small town in England can only be imagined.

The initial success of any attack at this stage of the war brought its own problems, contributing to the static nature of trench warfare. The beaten defenders would be forced back into relatively 'clean' ground where they could re-establish their defences. They would be bringing up supplies through the intact communication systems to their rear. If, as at Messines, they had lost only their front line, their second line of defence, reserve trenches and wire entanglements would still be in place. The attackers, however, would be trying to supply their troops and to consolidate their defences by bringing materials, weapons, food and men over the totally devastated battlefield. The 'Bite and Hold' strategy of which Plumer was an advocate, in which infantry would advance to take an objective behind an intense artillery barrage, then consolidate their positions and allow the enemy to exhaust himself with counter-attacks, was not so much a strategy as a necessity.

Plumer's troops stopped at the Messines Ridge. Progressing beyond the initial objective would have been suicidal and was only briefly considered by the General Staff. For more than seven weeks, the trenches on the ridge were modified and 'turned around' to defend against attacks from the east. Fresh wire entanglements were put in place and the supporting infrastructure, artillery and logistical support were moved forward to reflect the position of the new front line.

There was, however, a body of opinion which held that it might have been better to have continued with the momentum from that first attack and immediately pressed on while the Germans were in disarray, with their morale badly dented. It was realized, however, that the problems associated with a rapid advance might have brought disaster, perhaps even leading to the loss of any gains made so far.

After the success of Messines, the troops were in the 'hold' phase of the 'bite-and-hold' operation. Plumer had asked for a two-week delay before the next phase of the offensive east of Ypres in order to consolidate the positions. Haig gave responsibility for the next operation to Lieutenant-General Sir Hubert Gough and his Fifth Army (which, until October 1916, had been the Reserve Army). The transfer of troops and logistics stretched the requested two-week pause to nearly eight weeks.

All was in place on 31 July when the new offensive started. Field-Marshal Haig, determined to build on the success of the Battle of Messines by driving the Germans from the Ypres sector altogether, had set the final objective as the small village of Passchendaele, about seven miles (11km) east-north-east of Ypres. And then it started to rain.

It is, I think, sensible to insert a short interlude here, to try to show the tactical rationale behind the Battle of Passchendaele, or, to give it its proper name, the Third Battle of Ypres. The village of Passchendaele (Passendal) was of no great military significance in itself, but it stands on the slightly higher ground to the north-east of Ypres. Once it was taken, and apart from the advantages of having driven the enemy from the high ground that overlooked the Salient, there would be the enormous psychological boost of being able to see beyond the battlefields, across the green unspoiled plains of Belgium. Haig also hoped that if he broke through the German lines here, he could wheel left towards the Channel ports, disrupt the German U-boat operations from captured bases in Belgium, and change the course of the war in the Allies' favour. Not for the first time in that war, the mentality that considered that one more costly sacrifice would prove decisive came into play.

The battle itself, which lasted from 31 July to 10 November, actually consisted of a series of linked offensives, each one designed to wrest another piece of territory from the Germans. Messines was the precursor action that secured the high ground to the south and south-east of Ypres, and it was followed by the Battles of Pilckem Ridge, Langemarck, Menin Road, Polygon Wood, Broodseinde,

Poelcappelle, and the First and Second Battles of Passchendaele. Hundreds of thousands of soldiers on both sides died, and the very name 'Passchendaele' became a byword for the senseless waste of human life in a ruined landscape of mud and shell holes.

A post-Great War map showing the stages and gains of the Third Battle of Ypres, culminating with the capture of Passchendaele, July–November 1917.

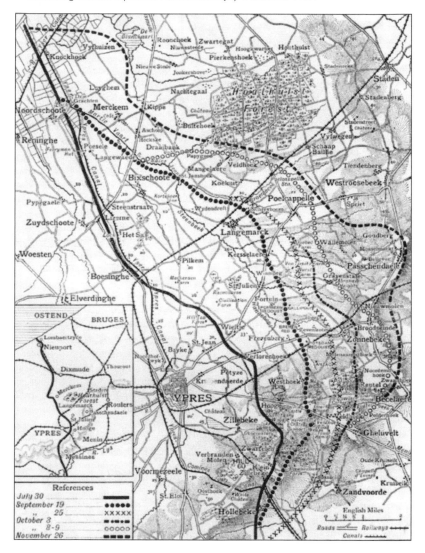

This period must have been a strange interval for the battalion. In late June, and during July and August, the 9th York and Lancasters saw little of the intense action that was continuing on the Ypres battlefield. The war diary gives an account of a unit moving from location to location behind the front line. They used the training areas and rifle ranges and, evidently, parade grounds. They marched, or were transported by lorries and trains. They stayed in billets, in tents and, at times, slept in the open.

Harry's story resumes on 10 June 1917, at the rest camp known as Scottish Lines, a relatively safe location about six miles (10km) behind the front lines.

The stay in 'the Lines' was only for a couple of days. On the 12th they had a short march to nearby Meteren, another hutted camp. Also about six miles behind the front line, Meteren at this time was a dedicated training area, with all the normal facilities – rifle ranges, assault courses and parade grounds, and for the next two weeks the battalion made good use of them. This was a rare opportunity to settle in and establish a comfortable billet. Captain A.W. Sykes, whom we will come across later, joined the battalion.

The end of June brings a chilling reminder of the reality of warfare. For the last four days of the month the 9th were back in the line at a location known as Hedge Street. The war diary simply indicates the location, relative to the line, of each of the four companies (Harry's C Company is in reserve.) An entry from that period concludes with: 'Situation normal. Casualties, officers – 2 officers killed, one wounded. O.R. 2 killed, 1 died of wounds, 12 wounded.' There is no mention of any raid or attack, by either side. 'Situation normal' – this was, simply, the casualty rate for four days in the front line. Casualties might result from shelling, sniper fire or maybe as a result of patrols or working parties venturing into no man's land. Harry will make a brief mention of these working parties in a letter to Kate in mid-July: 'we have had a rough time this last week or two going on working parties at night.' Clearly, being on one of these details was not a happy occupation.

Out of the line early in July, the battalion moved back to another training camp known as Micmac (the name of a Native American tribe), close to the modern village of Dikkebus (Dickebusch to the British in 1917), for more training and some reorganization. More than 260 new soldiers joined the battalion, replacing most of the 280 or so casualties incurred at Messines. Rugeley and the other training camps at home were delivering the goods.

There were occasional breaks in the routine of military life, as the war diary entry records, although the routine was soon re-established:

July 3rd-5th Bn at MICMAC camp. On the 4th inst. H.M. the King passed HALLEBAST CORNER at about 9.15 am. The Bn collected informally by the roadside to cheer the King.
B Coy and 85 ORs of C Coy proceeded to Battersea Farm on the 4th for work in the line for 2 days.

This location in the village of Zillebeke, about a mile (1.6km) from the front line, would have been as close to the trenches as the King's advisers would have allowed him to go. When first I came across this entry in the war diary I was surprised that Harry hadn't mentioned the event in one of his letters. He would surely have remembered seeing King George V and been keen to tell about it. But a more careful reading of the entry explains what must have happened. Harry missed the King because he was sent off to work in the line with most of C and all of B Company. Battersea Farm would have been quite familiar territory, less than a mile from the starting point for the Messines Ridge attack.

Harry sent a couple of letters to sister Kate in July, and then they simply stopped for quite a while. Some followers of the blog became quite concerned that he might have met with misfortune.

July 6 1917

Dear Kate

I have received your letter was very pleased with it. I have received some nice letters from Jack he seems in very good health only very busy. Letters are very nice out here. Don't send any cigs we get plenty out here you could send chocolate or biscuits anything to eat. envelopes about half a dozen. Ethel tells me Willie gets [is becoming] *a rum chap always running away and getting into things. Write back as soon as you receive this letter. Address 32507, 9th Batt York and Lancs C company L. G. Section 12 Platoon BEF France. I think this is all just now will write again soon*

yours truly

Harry

On the following day, the war diary records: '7th July The Bn less Bn HQ moved to the line on the night of 10/11th to work under supervision of the R.E.s [Royal Engineers] completing the work on the night of 12/13th.' For troops on the Western Front, a normal part of active service was to provide the labour for developing, strengthening or repairing the trench system. The soldiers would move up through the communication trenches to the front line (and sometimes beyond), work through the night as instructed by the Royal Engineers, and return before the dawn 'hate'. As has been said, for obvious reasons most activities in and about the trenches took place at night.

War diary, 14 July: 'The Battalion moved to billets in the STEENVOORDE area by motor lorry arriving in billets about 5 p.m.' Steenvoorde is about fifteen miles (24km) from the front line. Despite its Flemish-sounding name, it lies just over the border in France, a couple of miles west of Boescheppe, and, being so far from the fighting, would have been a haven after the last few weeks spent in and just behind the front line. There, the sound of the guns would have been only a distant rumble. On arriving, Harry wrote another letter to Kate.

July 14/1917

Dear Kate

I have received your parcel it came in very nice. we were just getting ready to move when I got it, we went in lorries so I did not have to carry it far I can tell you there was not much left as me and my pals were short and we could not get anything where we landed. It is a country place a few miles behind the firing line. The weather is lovely, we are all enjoying the ride. I'm in good health but we have had a rough time this last week or two going on working parties at night digging trenches and one thing and another. One night we were between our lines and the Germans but we all came out alright. It's a bit rough but it might be worse. My address is the same. Will write again soon. Glad to hear they are all right at home.

    Yours truly

    Harry

Evidently, the parcel contained some welcome food.

After that cheerful note to Kate there were no more letters from Harry until September. This led me to believe that he had been allowed leave at some time between the middle of July and the start of September. I had no 'hard' evidence, however, and it wasn't mentioned in any letter. But the circumstantial evidence was quite strong. In theory, soldiers were entitled to two weeks' leave each year. When and if it actually happened was something of a lottery, though, and very much depended upon the operational demands and the administrative efficiency of a soldier's unit.

For the rest of July, through August and into September, the battalion tramped around Flanders from billet to billet. There were short periods supporting the line, but mainly there was training, drill, and more drill and training. Soldiering in the Great War, as all soldiering, would seem to have consisted of short intervals of unbelievable terror separated by periods of utter boredom and pointless movement.

At this point we can pause to celebrate Harry's thirtieth birthday on 28 August 1917. The card from Willie and Connie (in Ethel's handwriting) is impressive, but it raised some real concerns when I came across it. It could hardly have survived the battlefield, or even just the general wear and tear of active service, in such excellent condition. On the other hand, if Harry was, as I then believed, home on leave at around the time of his birthday, he might have been given the card and then left it with Ethel for safekeeping when his leave ended and he returned to the front. This was,

Harry's thirtieth-birthday card from Connie and Willie, August 1917.

I thought, a reasonable theory, and would explain how the card came to survive. But it simply wasn't true. I later found out that Harry did not have any leave in the summer of 1917.

In the entire ninety-six days from 10 June to 15 September, the 9th Battalion, the York and Lancaster Regiment spent sixty-seven days 'housekeeping' and training, fourteen days moving – either marching or by lorry, four days allocated as rest days, and only ten days in the line or in direct support. In addition, on several nights some men of the battalion, including Harry, were allocated to working parties and sent forward to the front line, and sometimes into no man's land, to improve the defences or to patrol. These were unpleasant and dangerous jobs, as Harry mentions in his letter to Kate of 14 July.

We cannot learn too much from the two letters written in this period. Harry spent a few days in the line. He spent some time in reserve and some far behind the lines. He was sent forward to work on the trenches. These are bald facts – his letters, being so infrequent, are not helpful in fleshing out his story. Yet, reading the letters in conjunction with the war diary entries, it has proved possible to get some sort of picture of his experiences.

Meanwhile, as Harry and his battalion were tramping around

Western Flanders, the war continued. Specifically, in the Ypres sector it continued with a battle that ranks with the Somme as a byword for the horrors of the fighting on the Western Front: Passchendaele...

Throughout August and September 1917, the Third Battle of Ypres, usually referred to as Passchendaele, was in full flow. The main offensives in August took place to the east and north-east of the city of Ypres. The focus of the attack – or rather, series of attacks – was along a line that can be traced running eastwards through the modern locations of Pilkem, Langemark, Poelkappelle and Passendale. For the time being, however, Harry's battalion was spared. During this period, the 9th York and Lancasters were with the rest of Second Army in the sector to the south of the city, and therefore not engaged in the major offensives.

July had been a fine month. The good weather meant that preparations for the next phase, the next assault in Haig's plan, were able to continue. On the 16th an intense bombardment of the enemy lines to the north of Ypres started up. The shelling focused on a small rise known as Pilckem (Pilkem) Ridge, about three miles (5km) north of Ypres. In the next two weeks, the British guns fired over 4 million shells. (To get an idea of the scale of the bombardment, that works out at an almost unimaginable average of more than three shells every second for fourteen days and nights.)

The aim, of course, was to destroy the German defences in preparation for the assault. Yet once again the deep, well-prepared, strongly built and well-stocked dugouts effectively protected most of the defenders. Worse for the attackers, the Germans had developed the use of mutually supporting, machine-gun equipped pillboxes. The bombardment proved unable to destroy them, any more than it could destroy barbed-wire entanglements.

All was set for the offensive to begin on 31 July, and at 3.50 that morning the attack on Pilckem Ridge duly got under way. The weather had changed dramatically since Messines, however. From the start, fortune certainly did not favour the Allied attackers. Dawn on the 31st brought torrential rain that continued without respite for the next four days. The rain was to play a major role in the campaign, for what lay ahead, although no one yet knew it, was the wettest August-to-November period in that part of Flanders on record. The delay after Messines, from two weeks to seven, was to prove critical.

A significant by-product of the intense shelling and the rain – indeed, a significant factor in the battle – was the mud. (When I wrote earlier that the battle was in 'full flow', I used the wrong words. This battle did very little 'flowing'. The mud made almost any progress virtually impossible.) The ancient drainage systems of the area, some of them natural and some dating back to the Middle Ages, had been badly affected, and often destroyed, by the shelling, with the result that the whole battlefield, which was originally drained marshland, became a quagmire. Losses through this period mounted steadily, not just to enemy action. Untold numbers of men, unable to escape the mud through wounds or the enormous weight of equipment, simply sank into the morass and drowned. Many were never found. Men, horses, mules, field guns, limbers, wagons, lorries – the mud claimed victims wherever there was no solid footing.

Yet despite the rain and the mud, and the intact defences, the first day saw most objectives taken, although at a heavy cost. The Allies incurred 15,000 casualties on the first day, a figure that had risen to around 32,000 by 2 August (with twelve VCs being won), for a gain of about one and a quarter to two miles (2–3kms). Against such losses, the capacity of the Rugeley training camp, 12,500 men, begins to seem quite modest.

On 1 August, the London *Times* reported:

> *Both British and French troops gained further ground today along their new front in Belgium, in spite of the heavy rain, which, falling since early yesterday afternoon, has turned the battlefield into a sea of mud and rendered major operations impossible.*

The famous picture included here, taken on the same day as *The Times*'s report, shows a stretcher party struggling through the

A single stretcher carried by seven men, one of the enduring images of the Great War. The soldier nearest the camera is wearing shorts, mentioned by Harry in a letter.

mud. Seven men to carry a single casualty, where normally two stretcher-bearers would suffice.

The rain continued, the conditions worsened and the attack, after the first two days, ground to a halt. Yet despite these problems, the enormous losses and the serious doubts expressed by his staff, Haig steadfastly insisted that the operation should continue until the objectives were met. He even ignored General Gough's plea that operations in the conditions were impossible. For ever the optimist, Haig believed that the major breakthrough was always imminent.

CHAPTER 6

MID-SEPTEMBER 1917 ONWARDS

THE PACE OF WAR SHIFTED noticeably for Harry's battalion. From the middle of September 1917, the lead role in the Passchendaele offensive passed from the Fifth Army to General Plumer's Second Army. Harry's battalion was in the 23rd Division, part of that army. The troops who had 'enjoyed' such success at Messines Ridge moved into the line. Plumer's offensive started on 20 September. We can follow the war diary entries and Harry's letters to get a picture of the reality of those events for the ordinary soldier.

On the 23rd Harry wrote to Jack:

September 23rd 1917.

Dear Jack

I have received your letter and I got the cigs alright. You did not mention about the mug you had got for Willie it will be very nice. I will tell Ethel he has to use it. The raid you read about in the papers was made by our Battalion. B Coy went over and we, no 12 platoon C Coy stood to [i.e. in support, if needed]. It was made to get a prisoner or two, to get information which they did, they lost one man and two wounded, it happened about five one morning. I got a slight wound in the face with shrapnel but not much it is alright now, I did not go to the doctor. There as been a big advance this last day or two but I have been left out. We get left out in turns. we are expecting our Coy out tonight. We have some rough times out here but I think the Germans have it rougher. We have to make the best of it. I should be glad when it is all over. John Bull watched us march past just over a week ago on our way to the trenches. I think we were the best batt in the Brigade, well in the division. I am pleased you're keeping well and that they are keeping well at home. The rations have been very low lately, four and five to a loaf and small loaves too, that is the days bread. Write back as soon as possible, I'm always pleased to get a letter from you. Kate keeps sending me small parcels which come is very nice, I hope she gets on alright at her fresh situation. I'm just going to write to Ethel.

With best love

Harry

Pages from the battalion war diary of the 9th York and Lancasters, including the entry for the start of the offensive on 20 September 1917.

Harry gives a very low-key description of some intense action. The war diary's description and the casualty figures give a much fuller picture:

20th [September] *ATTACK DAY: at zero hour, 5.40 am A Coy lost 22 killed & wounded. 3 Coys & Batt HQ went into tunnels. 1 Coy in trenches on top: about 1 P.M.* C *Coy* [Harry's company] *went forward to reinforce 68th Bde and dug in rear of BLUE LINE nr JASPER TRENCH: 4.30 Batt ordered to relieve 10th N.F.s* [Northumberland Fusiliers] *in BLUE LINE: 5.45 pm to 7 pm terrific shelling: relief complete 10 pm.*

20th–21st night Coys digging the whole night & by morning all coys had a continuous line of trench: B Coy formed defensive flank from right of 13th D.L.I. [Durham Light Infantry] *to left of 41st Div. 21st Very heavy shelling throughout the day. 6.30 p.m. Enemy counter-attack: C Coy moved forward to strengthen B Coy: Enemy did not reach our lines.*

22nd Very misty morning: enemy shelling heavy especially near Batt H.Q.; continual enemy sniping from TOWER HAMLETS. 6 p.m. to 8 p.m. hurricane bombardment of our supports & defensive flank.

The 'ATTACK DAY' in the war diary is a different operation to the 'raid' that Harry refers to in his letter to Jack. A Company suffered twenty-two casualties, whereas Harry refers to B Company 'going over' in a raid and losing one man killed and two wounded. At any one time there might be several operations going on simultaneously within the battalion.

Plumer's offensive on 20 September set three objectives for the assault, each marked with a series of coloured lines on the trench maps issued to the attacking units and supporting arms. The sequence was Red, Blue, then Green Lines, with the Blue Line close to Polygon Wood on the Menin Road.

Tough times on the 20th and 21st. Most of the battalion would have spent the night digging trenches, only to spend the next day under heavy shellfire. B Company in the front line would have been pleased that the job had been finished during the previous night.

On the 21st, Harry's C Company was sent to strengthen the front line when the enemy counter-attacked. The 'heavy shelling' mentioned in the war diary may have been responsible for Harry's 'slight wound in the face with shrapnel but not much'. By now we have learned that he is not a man to make a fuss. As to the German counter-attack, the war diary remarks laconically, 'Enemy did not reach our lines.' The attackers were beaten off. Some of the German troops would have been shelled as they advanced. The normal routine for a front-line unit, on spotting an enemy attack, was immediately to call for artillery support to try to break up the attack at an early stage. If, on the 21st that had not been completely effective, then it is quite possible that Harry's Lewis-gun team would have put their training to use, with some effect.

Food was tremendously important to the troops in the trenches. Since they were often cold, wet and muddy, and frequently very tired, it was understandable that they would think of hearty meals, thick soups and stews, to fortify them against the elements. The reality, of course, was that almost the only edible treats came from their food parcels. Extra food from home was welcome as a supplement to the very poor rations that they were expected to live off. Bread was an essential, but as we have seen, it was usually far from being very fresh. Now we learn that the quantities were a real problem at this time. A shared loaf of stale bread between four or five – and Harry notes that it is a small loaf – is not exactly fighting fare. The bread would be supplemented by tinned 'bully beef' (from French boeuf bouilli, boiled beef – i.e. corned beef, 'corned' meaning cured with salt), tea and endless cigarettes. Furthermore, delivering hot food to the front line could be a real problem. The cooking facilities might be a mile or so behind the lines and the hay boxes used to keep the food hot while it was transported were simply that – wooden boxes lined with hay. Sometimes, for any one of a number of reasons, hot food would not arrive in the front-line trenches, and the soldiers would resort to eating anything they had cold, often bully beef with hard biscuits or Maconochie straight from the tin, supplemented with anything they might have left over from their parcels. Tea, though, they could usually rustle up, heating the water on braziers or small spirit stoves.

Harry, very politely, frequently reminds Kate and Jack how much he appreciates their parcels. It is clear from his letters that he would, as was the normal practice, share his 'extras' with his pals. He would expect to share in their good fortune whenever it came around, and no doubt did.

We learn from his letter to Kate that Harry is about to write to his wife Ethel, and she plainly wrote to him, as can be seen from references he makes in his letters to Jack and Kate. The letters to Ethel have not survived, however. In some ways I am grateful that I don't have to make any decision about publishing what was surely very personal and possibly intimate correspondence. I have been told that Ethel was extremely upset by the war and everything to do with it. I am not sure of the reasons behind this, but the upshot was that she destroyed all the letters. It may be that she was a little less bitter by the time the 'Jack and Kate' letters came to her in the 1940s, which perhaps explains why she did not destroy those as well.

Before the battalion went back into the line on 20 September, it had been sent to an assembly point, as the war diary attests: '19th Moved from camp at 9.45 pm to BEDFORD HOUSE being "A" Battn of Reserve Brigade.'

Bedford House was the name the British gave to Château Rosandel when it was first taken over as a command post. The château building had been destroyed by shelling during the course of the fighting in the Salient, but the deep, secure cellars continued to be used as a headquarters. It is easily found today, situated on the main road, the N336, about two miles (3km) to the south of Ypres. The grounds are now a war cemetery but, visiting it today, it is just possible to see the remains of the château. The old moat frames a beautiful and tranquil setting, immaculately maintained, as these places always are, by the Commonwealth War Graves Commission. Since the British front line at this time would have been a little over a mile away from Bedford House, it was an ideal stopping-off and assembly point for troops moving forward, or for regrouping on return.

On the Ypres battlefield as a whole, the distances involved are surprisingly small. The Dickebusch training area, the battalion's last stop before Bedford House, was just over two miles (4km) to the west of Ypres. Mount Sorrel, their objective at Messines Ridge, was as far again to the east. The Menin Road, the focus for much of the action in the coming few weeks, with 'Hellfire Corner', is about two miles to the north-east. 'Hellfire Corner', the junction of the

The cemetery at Bedford House today, seen from the road and showing part of the old moat of the château that had stood there until the war came.

Menin Road with a railway line, provided a perfect 'bullseye' for the German artillery. The area was pre-registered on their guns, so as soon as any activity was noted there, a few shells could be sent on their way. It was not a place to linger in. The standard practice was to get through it as quickly as possible by whatever means of transport – foot, horse, motor – was being used.

The area today is, of course, very different from how it was in the autumn of 1917. Trees, hedges and undergrowth dominate the landscape, where Harry would have seen a shell-pocked morass of mud, littered with the debris of warfare. There would be nothing but desolation between the two front lines. The war diary takes up the account following the actions on 20–22 September:

> *23rd [September] Misty: protective barrage 5.30 a.m. Heavy bursts of enemy artillery throughout the day.*
> *24th Protective barrage in early morning: heavy enemy shelling 5.15 a.m. to 7 a.m.: 6 p.m. to 7.30 p.m.*
> *24th–25th night relieved by 11th SUSSEX [Royal Sussex Regiment]: relief complete 8.45 p.m. Enemy got to know of our relief and shelled heavily. Casualties during tour: Officers, killed 1, wnd 7: O.R.'s killed 22 wounded 83, missing 4.*

It would appear from his next letter (see p.81) that Harry missed this uncomfortable couple of days, having been detached from the battalion and sent, presumably with a working party, to help shift artillery. He met with some interesting experiences on the 25th or 26th, as he was to recount to Jack. Things became even more interesting, however, after he returned from the working party to the front-line trenches, as the war diary reports:

25th Batt at CHIPPAWA CAMP [Chippewa: another Native American tribe] *cleaning, reorganizing etc.*

26th Inspection by Divisional General.

27th Proceeded to RIDGE WOOD, arr 5 pm.

28th 10.00 am to BEDFORD HOUSE. 8.30 pm ordered to relieve 8th KOYLI [King's Own Yorkshire Light Infantry] *in front line.*

29th relief complete about 10 pm: took over right sector, right Brigade: relief slightly delayed by shelling. DISPOSITIONS: front line C Coy: close support A Coy less 2 platoons: counter-attack coy, D Coy: Batt reserve, 2 platoons A Coy & 2 plats B Coy: Gen reserve, B Coy less 2 platoons.

30th About 4 am very thick mist; 4.30 am intense bombardment helped on with minenwerfers [German trench mortars] *& smoke bombs: 5.15 am enemy discovered in large numbers advancing against our trench especially on our right: mist still very thick: enemy used bombs and flammenwerfer* [flamethrowers]. *Heavy fire with rifles, Lewis machine guns and bombs was opened on them & none reached our trench: S.O.S. sent up but was not seen at Batt H.Q. owing to mist: an orderly arrived with the first news at 7.20 am. About 6 am enemy again attacked but was driven off: took 2 prisoners, 1 flammenwerfer & a machine gun: 60 or 70 dead were left in front of our trenches: the attack was repulsed entirely with the fire of the infantry: the artillery did not barrage our front: a wire fence, put up during the previous night by a pioneer battn helped greatly to impede the enemy. A short barrage was put down on our lines at 10 am: the remainder of the day was normal.*

The location of all this action is likely to have been on the south side of the Menin Road, close to the hamlet of Gheluvelt (Geluveld).

The war diary entry for the following two days also makes interesting reading:

Menin Road

1st [October] *During night Sept 30th–Oct 1st front line garrison was increased by 3 sections & wire was repaired. 5 am to 6 am heavy enemy shelling: our protective barrage opened at 5.15 am. S.O.S. went up on our left at 6am but no infantry action followed on our front. Heavily shelled about 12.30 pm especially round Batt H.Q. Enemy aeroplanes active all day flying low and firing: fire was opened from the ground but without effect. 6.30 pm enemy bombarded & at 7 pm was seen massing: the artillery put down the barrage promptly in reply to our S.O.S. & quashed the attack; after this, the night was quiet.*

2nd Protective barrage at dawn. Intermittent shelling during the day. Relieved by 1st R. West Kents [Royal West Kent Regiment]. *Relief complete 11.45 pm.*

Casualties during tour killed 1 officer 3 O.R. Wounded 3 officers 22 O.R.s: Missing 3 O.R.s.

Harry takes up the account of the German assault on the 30th:

3rd October 1917

Dear Jack

Just a line to let you know I'm going on all right. In my last letter I told you we was waiting for the lads coming out well that night I had to go up the line to help them out with the guns. we brought them part way in the lumber waggons on the way we had a smash a motor lorry ran into us smashed the wheels of the lumber wagon and tipped us all out but we only got a few bumps which we are used to. Three days after, we were called up the line again of course I went this time. We had to go to the front line were it was on the Menin Road no doubt you have heard about it. We were there for three days it was awful the shelling day and night. We relieved the KOYLI about 10 o'clock

General Service wagons taking ammunition along the Menin Road, east of Ypres, in the autumn of 1917. Harry was involved in a 'smash' with a motor lorry while with a working party that was being transported by a GS wagon.

and what do you think Fritz came over about 5 o'clock next morning we had an exciting time for about one hour and a half I can tell you. but we beat him off he never got in our trenches he was about two hundred strong it was a picked storming party so the prisoners say that captured, they brought liquid fire [flamethrowers] *with them and bombs and all sorts but not many got back we had twenty casuals and the captain got killed a jolly good fellow too. I was pleased to get out of it but did not feel nervous when I saw them coming over. No 1 in our section was on the gun and we used our rifles. Our Coy as to go before the* [divisional] *general for the good work we have done. We have just been given a long trousers again as we have had short ones all summer. I hope you are going on alright as was pleased to hear you are keeping in good health, write again as soon as possible. I am always ready for a letter. I think the mug will be very nice for Willie*

With best love
Harry

Harry, for once, gives a very clear account of the events of 29 and 30 September in this latest letter to Jack. He seems to have had quite an adventure a few days before. The 'lumber waggons' would be the standard horse-drawn, open-bodied, four-wheeled general-service (GS) wagons designed for transporting the tons of timber, ammunition, barbed wire, equipment and pretty much anything else used in trench warfare. Built of wood with metal fittings, they had spoked and iron-rimmed wooden wheels.

Even at this stage of the war, horse-drawn transport was still the main method of moving equipment, including artillery. The advantages of the motor lorry were just beginning to be realized; meanwhile, the horses suffered dreadfully. The two technologies collide – literally, in Harry's experience.

The enemy's counter-attack on the morning of the 30th was a

A German 77-mm *Minenwerfer* (trench mortar) and crew on the Western Front. They are clearly not in action: the men have no helmets, and the weapon has been lowered from the high angle at which it was usually fired.

major action, and Harry was at the centre of it. The Germans had lost ground over the recent weeks and were becoming demoralized. Their carefully prepared defences were – despite the interlocking pillboxes, the well-constructed trenches prepared in depth, the wire entanglements and the mud – falling to the determined (if costly) Allied assaults. This counter-attack against the 9th York and Lancasters was important, and the preparation for it would have been meticulous. At five o'clock in the morning it would have been dark, the visibility worsened by a thick mist lying over the battlefield.

The assault began with an 'intense [artillery] bombardment helped on with minenwerfers & smoke bombs'. There is no way of telling how long the enemy bombardment would have lasted. The minenwerfer was a short-range weapon, and would certainly have been fired from the enemy's front line directly ahead. Possibly they caused the casualties among the battalion rather than rifle and machine-gun fire during the assault. The whole performance, rather more than the normal morning's 'hate', would have meant that the British troops, already 'stood to' at that time of day, would have been on guard for an attack.

When the attacking German infantry were spotted (I have no idea how the defenders would see – darkness, mist and smoke bombs must have made observation challenging, at the least), following standard procedure a flare was sent up as an SOS, to call up artillery support. But at 5.15 a.m., in the poor conditions, nobody saw the flare, and so the battalion was left on its own, to deal with the attack as best it could.

They did well. Harry's letter to Jack of 3 October was the first, years ago, to catch my attention among the bundle in the drawer, describing the attack and his feelings. What struck me especially was the line 'I . . . did not feel nervous when I saw them coming over.' In this, perhaps, lies a clue to the nature of the British infantry of the Great War, men who faced danger and privation and terrible risks with a simple acceptance of reality and an unflinching shrug at their fate and their duty. Earlier in the same letter Harry writes, 'we only got a few bumps which we are used to.' There is a wealth of character in that simple, understated aside.

The censor's handiwork on Harry's letter to Kate of 3 October 1917.

Harry mentions the action to Kate, giving away much more military information than he normally did in letters to his sister, although still much less detail than in the letter to Jack.

Oct 3rd

Dear Kate,

Just a line to let you know I'm going on alright. We had an exciting time and this time up the line. We had only been in about six hours when fritz's came over to us. We had an hour and a half of it but we beat them back and they lost a good many men too not many got back I can tell you. We lost —————— [pencilled out; probably censored] which I'm sorry to say and about ————————— wounded. I think the mug will be all right for Willie which Jack is getting for him. If you send me anything it will come in very nice the chocolate is very good I should like a bit of cake, if you could afford it really gets crushed so if it is not packed careful. Write as soon as possible. I hope you'll get on alright at your fresh place
with best love from
Harry

This letter shows the only clear evidence of censorship to be found in any of Harry's letters. The casualty figures have been firmly and effectively obliterated with a soft pencil and are unreadable.

Soldiers' letters were censored usually by a company or battalion officer, a job that most officers loathed. Quite apart from the time it took, they disliked reading personal and sometimes intimate details that they regarded as private to the sender. Military censors employed in rear areas at field post offices tended to be rather less sympathetic, however.

By great good fortune (and a good illustration of the power of the Internet), I have been able to obtain an account from the German viewpoint. One of the followers of Harry's blog, Bob Lembke, has a special interest in the German flamethrower detachments. His father had been a member of one of these units, and Bob has kindly sent me this short account:

The Death Book of the German Flamethrower Regiment, a Prussian Guard unit sponsored by the Kaiser and [his son] the Prussian Crown Prince, indicates that two flame pioneer privates died fighting in Flanders on that day. I must comment that this death roll must be very accurate; the commander of the regiment, Major Dr Reddemann, had to report to the highest Army Command . . .

The death roll states that Flamen Pioniere Paul Kraus and Friedrich Maas fell in Flanders that day. . . . As one flamethrower was found on the battlefield [captured by the 9th York and Lancasters], which the Germans tried hard to prevent, it is likely that the two privates were the two-man crew of the flamethrower, which almost certainly would have been the Wex model, a very sophisticated design . . .

Generally flame attacks took two forms, one being perhaps two or four devices advancing with extreme stealth; or, alternatively, of massed devices (sometimes thirty or sixty or more) attacking suddenly, the shock effect of the surprise mass attack and the manner in which the smoke of the devices screened the operators from counter-fire often leading to a complete if local breakdown of the defence. This attack seems to have been neither, probably leading to the failure of the attack. Over the entire war, Dr Reddemann's statistics indicate that 82 per cent of these attacks were 'successful' . . . (Most of the [German] dead in this attack must have been supporting infantry.)

From Bob Lembke's detailed knowledge, it does seem certain that the flamethrower units were only used in circumstances where success was extremely likely (hence the 82 per cent success rate). Harry and his comrades were fortunate to have come through this ordeal mainly unscathed.

A contemporary account of the day's action almost certainly refers to the attack on Harry's trenches:

Passchendaele Sept 30th
Early this morning the enemy heavily bombarded our positions between
Tower Hamlets and Polygon Wood, and subsequently launched three
attacks, all of which were repulsed with loss. The first attack, delivered
south of the Reutelbeek, was beaten off by our fire before reaching our
position. Shortly afterwards hostile infantry advanced astride the Ypres-
Menin road under cover of a thick smoke barrage and accompanied
by Flammenwerfer detachments, and succeeded temporarily in driving
in one of our advanced posts. An immediate counter-attack by our
troops recaptured the post together with a number of prisoners and
machine-guns. Later; in the morning an attempt to repeat this attack
was broken up by our artillery fire.

This card (below) was included among the letters, although
I don't know to whom Harry sent it. It commemorates 23rd
Division's action. I can find a record of the artist, J.V. Breffit, not
as an artist, but as an Army officer. The date, 20 September, was
the start of the Battle of the Menin Road – another step in the
advance astride that road towards Passchendaele.

The loss of Harry's company commander in the action on 30
September – 'the captain got killed' – initiated some detective
work. One of the purposes behind a visit I made to the Flanders
battlefields, with others, in the
summer of 2008, was identifying
this officer and locating his
grave. Since searching the many
cemeteries in the area appeared a
daunting task, it seemed sensible
to start with the Bedford House
Cemetery. There are more
than a thousand graves in the
cemetery, but luck was on our
side. As soon as we located the
date area for September 1917,
there he was: 'Captain A. W.
Sykes, York & Lancaster Regt.,

'The captain got killed a jolly good fellow too' – Captain Sykes's gravestone in Bedford House Cemetery.

30th September 1917 Age 42. The dearly loved husband of Mary Sykes, Netherleigh, Huddersfield'.

I was initially a little hesitant about the identification, as the war diary entry for June 25 reported Captain Sykes as joining the battalion and being posted to A Company. Yet since there was only one officer killed on that tour in the front line (29 September–2 October), he must have been given temporary command of C Company. Harry's epitaph for him – 'a jolly good fellow too' – is the more eloquent for its simplicity and obvious sincerity.

Whatever the event, or the casualties, the battalion, caught up in the huge war machine, carried on as usual. The war diary entry states that on 3 October 'Battalion moved to METEREN area by bus, embussing at 2pm and arriving in billets by 6pm.' This was a return to the familiar training area west of Ypres. For the soldiers it meant relief from the trenches, with the opportunity to write letters and perform many other tasks: wash themselves and their clothes, dry and clean weapons and other equipment, delouse themselves and their uniforms – even catch up on some sleep, if drill and training permitted. In the end, the respite lasted a week. The war diary takes up the narrative:

> 5th *The Commanding Officer inspected the Bn. on the 5th inst.* [i.e. of the current month].
> 2nd Lt D H WEBBE *was transferred to England & struck off the strength. Capt C Palmer ordered* [to attend] *a Medical Board and also struck off (Authy A G No D/1981).*
> 10th *At 2pm the Bn moved to the front line and relieved the 11th Bn W.Yorks.*
> 11 to 14 [October] *Casualties Capt. S. Riddell killed 2Lts A. J. Walters & R Coyles wounded. 12 O.R. killed 77 OR wounded 4 OR missing believed killed.*
> *Night of 14th to MICMAC camp.*

[The war diary then lists what has happened to four officers wounded before the latest tour in the front line] *Major Gylls A.R. wounded to England 1-10-17. 2Lt A Barber ditto 2-10-17. 2Lt H G Smith ditto 29-9-17 2Lt J.E. Hall ditto 25-9-17*

There must be an explanation for the heavy casualties suffered between 11 and 14 October, but the battalion war diary merely records the losses in officers and men for the battalion's stint in the front line. There is absolutely no account of any action, or even of any notable events, on those days.

The casualties were heavy. Around 10 per cent of the notional strength were killed or wounded – over four times the losses in the action of 30 September–2 October, for which the war diary provides a relatively detailed account.

On 12 October, while the battalion was in the front line, the next stage of the advance was launched, the main assault carried out this time by Australian and New Zealand troops. Their losses were enormous, though they met with little success. The 9th York and Lancasters must have been incidental to the main attack, yet the battalion drew significant casualties from the fighting resulting from it.

After the relatively dry September, the wet weather had emphatically returned. In the two days up to 9 October an inch (25mm) of rain had fallen, over half the normal rainfall for the month. The whole battlefield became a sea of mud. October 1917 was thought to be the wettest October in Flanders that century.

Two extracts from contemporary accounts of the events may help us to understand something of this terrible time. The first, from a New Zealander, is recorded on the 'Flanders 1917' website (www.flanders1917.info):

Recovering the New Zealand wounded from the battlefield took two and a half days even with 3,000 extra men . . . The conditions were horrendous and up to eight men were needed to carry each stretcher because of the mud and water. The Germans suffered the same problems and an informal truce for stretcher-bearers came into force, although anyone without a stretcher was fired on. By the evening of October 14 there simply was no one left alive on the battlefield.

Field Marshal Sir Douglas Haig's account of the battle paints a sorry picture of brave men engaged in a futile task:

They advanced every time with absolute confidence in their power to overcome the enemy, even though they had sometimes to struggle through mud up to their waists to reach him. So long as they could reach him they did overcome him, but physical exhaustion placed narrow limits on the depth to which each advance could be pushed, and compelled long pauses between the advances.

Although not engaged in the main push, there was little respite for the 9th York and Lancasters, as the war diary records (the curious combinations of letters and figures, such as 'J11a', are map references):

15 & 16 [October] *MICMAC CAMP. Cleaning up: C. O.'s inspection. 2Lt A J Walker died of wounds 16th: Capt S. W. Wicks hosp*[italized] *sick 16th.*
17 Relieved 11 W Yorks in reserve Zillebeke Bund about 5.30 pm
18 Batt moved to line and relieved 8 KOYLI. 2 Lt Wheliker to England.
20 Batt relieved by 11 W Yorks. Batt H. Q. B & D Coys to BUND: A Coy relieved Coy of 11 WY[orks] *nr J11a & became support coy to 8 York* [Yorkshire Regiment; generally known as the Green Howards]*: C Coy to bout Jsc in support to 11 WY. Total casualties for tour 4 O.R. killed, 20 O.R. wounded.*
21 To Brewery Camp.

Once again, the casualties are recorded without comment. These losses would have been considered 'normal' for three days in the front line at a time of much activity.

From 21 October, the battalion moved away from the front line and returned to rest, recuperation and routine training. Harry's letter to Jack a few days later sums up his experiences and adds some pleasant personal details. We get a picture of the comradeship and sharing that were so valued among the soldiers, and we can see that winning a medal was not high among his priorities. Willie's mug figures again, and we learn that Harry, clearly, had been enjoying married life before the war interfered. At the end of the month, two of the top brass visited for inspections. On the 29th the divisional commander, Major-General Babington, inspected the battalion. Two days later, the Commander-in-Chief,

Sir Douglas Haig, inspected the brigade. I would guess that it was Babington who spoke to C Company, rather than Haig himself.

Dear Jack,

I was very pleased to have another letter from you I have not had many lately. I have not heard from Kate yet will you send me her address at once I think some of her letters must have got lost. We have had a busy time in the trenches since seventeenth of September till just now. We are out for a rest we have earned it we were in the trenches five Sundays out of six so you can tell, we want another draft [of replacements] *now there is not many left now. I think there is more military medals in our company than any other in France. No 1 & 2 in our gun team has got one so you see we are proud. The General said we can't all get them if we earn them but I'm alright and I don't bother about one. There is above twenty in our company now with them, as long as I am alright I don't care. I was going up to the trenches last month and on the road got talking to an artillery man. It come too his home was in Oxford. he said there was some East Oxford lads with him. I told him my name but he did not know me as he went to school at Henley. He gave me a packet of chocolate a package of cigs box of matches and two candles not a bad sort what you think. The pillbox we took over was one the Australians had taken a day or two before. The Germans would not come out so they burnt them out it was in a state. We have been on the range today firing. I did not do at all bad only I am not much good at rapid firing but at 300 yards application, fires* [fire as] *you like, plenty of time I got 19 points out of 20 4 bulls and one inner. I was very pleased to hear that you are thinking of getting married. I should not wait a day. I should not like to be single again and I think that you will say the same let me know as soon as possible. They tell me Willie likes his mug and is very pleased with it. I got your packet alright. I should be glad when the war is over so that I can come and see you. Don't forget Kate's address when you write and write soon yourself*
with best love from
    Harry

'I died in Hell' – dead and badly wounded British soldiers during the fighting for Passchendaele. This photograph was taken by Frank Hurley, famous for the images he took during Shackleton's Antarctic expedition of 1914–17.

The letter is undated, but by referring to the battalion war diary it is possible to date it with some confidence to 27 October – the day on the rifle range.

Almost certainly the Lewis gun No.1 and No. 2 were awarded their Military Medals for the action on 30 September. Without their names and a specific mention in the war diary, however, it has not been possible to uncover any citation. I would also have liked to have been able to identify the pillbox that seems to have been taken with a flamethrower, or possibly phosphorus grenades (P bombs), but, without a specific date, it proved impossible. The Australians cleared many pillboxes on the road to Passchendaele.

On the day after Harry wrote to Jack, a brief entry in the war diary signalled an enormous change for him and his comrades.

28 To billets in Wizennes [Wizernes] 2.15 pm arrived 5 pm. instructions recvd to recall all men on leave, courses etc.

The Passchendaele offensive as a whole lasted from 31 July to 10 November. Despite the fine spell in September, what is chiefly remembered about the battle (or series of battles, really), other than the enormous casualties, is the misery of fighting in mud and water. The area to the north of the Menin Road had been a marsh before ever the battle started. The bombardment and the rain simply combined to produce a morass of almost impassable mud.

After five months of heavy fighting, Canadian troops finally took the village of Passchendaele on 6 November. By then, the once substantial village had been reduced to a smear of rubble and brick dust in a sea of mud and shell holes. The cost had been immense. The Allies had sustained almost half a million casualties, while the Germans reported just over a quarter of a million men killed or seriously wounded. For the Allies, a gain of around five miles (8km), capturing the high ground around Ypres, had cost 140,000 lives. Yet despite this cost in lives and the suffering of the troops, the Allies were forced to withdraw from the high ground just four months later, virtually back to their original line.

This 'last-push-to-achieve-a-breakthrough' philosophy permanently damaged Haig's reputation. The huge losses to achieve little of any importance, and his determination to persist with the offensive in such terrible conditions, were unforgivable.

There are many accounts of Passchendaele by those who survived it. The overall German commander in the sector, General Erich Ludendorff, shows nothing but admiration for the men of both sides:

The horror of the shell-hole area of Verdun [February–December 1916] *was surpassed. It was no longer life at all. It was mere unspeakable suffering. And through this world of mud the attackers dragged themselves, slowly, but steadily, and in dense masses. Caught in the advanced zone by our hail of fire they often collapsed, and the lonely man in the shell-hole breathed again. Then the mass came on again. Rifle and machine-gun jammed with the mud. Man fought against man, and only too often the mass was successful.*

More succinct, but no less telling, is a line from the war poet Siegfried Sassoon, who served on the Western Front as an officer of the Royal Welch Fusiliers:

I died in Hell – (They called it Passchendaele).

CHAPTER 7

THE JOURNEY TO ITALY

AFTER A VERY UNPLEASANT time in or close to the front line, Harry's battalion moves away to regroup and reorganize. The war diary for the last three days of October reports the arrival of three separate drafts, totalling 220 soldiers, replacing casualties, which need to be absorbed into the unit. After being relieved in the front line on 20 October, the battalion spends a day in Brewery Camp 'cleaning up' before moving by train to Wizernes, a training camp in France some thirty miles (48km) west of the front line at Ypres. For the next three weeks, they spend their time cleaning, training and generally sorting out in the relative calm of the Wizernes training area.

The war diary for the period has some interesting entries:

29 G.O.C. Div [general officer commanding the division] *inspected batt 10 a.m. draft of 95 O.R. joined.*
30 range practice for the draft; cleaning up etc. for C in C's [commander-in-chief's] *inspection. 2Lt W T S Smith joined.*
31 C in C inspected the Brigade
drafts of 50 O.Rs & 75 O.R.s joined.

As early as 28 October, the 23rd Division, along with four other British divisions, had received orders to prepare to move to an unknown destination. It is these orders that would have triggered the recall of personnel. At that date, five divisions would have totalled well over 50,000 men. Their departure from the front would have put more pressure on the remaining troops in the sector.

Field Marshal Haig inspected the division at Leulinghem, near Wizernes, on the 31st. It is a widely held view that Haig never actually saw the front line in all his time as Commander-in-Chief on the Western Front. His entire appreciation of the state of the soldiers under his command and the conditions they were enduring was based entirely on reports from his staff. His own assessment of the Passchendaele offensive, reported near the end of the last chapter (pp. 90–1), was a condensed version of reports he had received. Harry's letters make no mention of his inspection.

The war diary continues:

November 1917 Wizernes
1st to 9th During this period the Battalion carried out a satisfactory training programme, and the specialists were trained by their own officers. Range practices were fired on the 1st 3rd 4th 6th & 7th the shooting was very satisfactory, and the men of the new drafts showed improvement. The Divl [Divisional] Gas officer inspected SBRs on the 2nd and lectured to all officers and Platoon Commanders on the 6th. A Church parade was held on the 4th. A draft of 50 ORs joined on the 5th inst and were inspected by the G.O.C. on the 8th. Whilst in this area there was very little sickness in the Battalion and the men benefitted from the rest.
Capt G A Crowther & 2Lt R C M Douthwaite returned from leave on the 1st having been recalled by wire [telegram]. 2nd Lt A.C Doc & E H Thompson MC rejoined from hospital on the 2nd. Lt Col Rumford DSO MC [the battalion CO] proceeded on leave to England on the 3rd and returned on the 6th. 2Lts L A Floyd, N A Dixon and Ward joined the Bn on the 3rd.
No. 15431 L/C [Lance-Corporal] Walker F was awarded the MM [Military Medal] for gallantry in the field. (DRO 3027 1/11/17). The G.O.C. remitted suspended sentence of 3 years Penal servitude in the Case of No 3141 Pte (a/L.Cpl) G R Worthington for an act of gallantry for which this man was awarded the MM and for continuous good behaviour & devotion to duty during the past three ms [months].

This 'block entry' covering nine days mentions the commanding officer heading off for leave in England for just three days. Most of that time would have been spent travelling. Two more drafts, of 95 and 50 soldiers, joined, making a total, in three weeks, of 270 new men to be absorbed into the battalion.

The story of Acting Lance-Corporal Worthington is intriguing. What did he do to earn three years' penal servitude? (Which may well have been a softer option than the Flanders trenches – perhaps a reason why the sentence was suspended and he returned to duty in the front line.) What did he do to earn his Military Medal? Sadly, the war diary gives no other details.

As intense as the fighting was in Flanders, there was a serious problem further to the south and east, in a different theatre of operations. In north-east Italy, the Austro-Hungarian Army, supported by German units and with its High Command bolstered by German commanders and advisers, had broken the resolve of the Italian Army at Caporetto and its troops were advancing, virtually unopposed, across the Venetian Plain.

Italian losses were enormous: 11,000 men were killed, 20,000 wounded and 275,000 taken prisoner; additionally, 2,500 guns were captured by the Austrians. Between 24 October and 9 November 1917 the Austro-Hungarian and German forces advanced more than 100 miles (160km) in the direction of Venice. They were only stopped at the Piave River, where the Italians (supported by French and British forces) established a new defensive line. Luckily for the Allies, the Austro-Hungarian support systems could not sustain such rapid progress, and it became necessary for the advancing army to pause to consolidate. The advance was halted by 10 November, as the 9th York and Lancasters set off from Flanders towards this fresh and very different theatre. On that day, the 23rd Division began the lengthy move by rail to Italy. The battalion war diary gives bare details of the journey:

10 [November] *The Bn entrained by half Battalion at WIZERNES STATION train no. 51 departed at 10.30 am. Lt Col Rumbold DSO MC being OC Train; Train no 54 left at 2.40pm with Major Lewis MC as OC train.*

11 to 15 Train through the RHONE valley to MARSEILLES and along the coast via CANNES, NICE & VINTIMILLE [Ventimiglia] *into ITALY. Halts repas* [haltes repas – meal stops] *were arranged at various stations, where men were exercised and hot water tea coffee were available. The train discipline was excellent and*

the men were interested throughout the journey. The Bn was warmly
welcomed en route. On the 15th the Bn detrained at MANTOVA
[Mantua] *and marched to CERESA.*

From the limited details in the war diary, the train seems likely
to have taken the troops, via Paris, south along the route of the
current high-speed train (TGV) track, through Lyons, down
the Rhône Valley to Arles. It would then have turned east and
followed the coastline to Marseilles, Cannes and Nice, and on to
Italy. The train would have crossed the border into Italy just west of
Ventomiglia and then passed through Genoa and Cremona before
arriving at its destination, Mantua, which lies about seventy-five
miles (120km) west-south-west of Venice. The march to Ceresa
was only about three miles (5km) and, after five days on the train,
should have presented no problems.

The total distance travelled was about a thousand miles
(1,600km). Five days' travel gives an average progress of 200
(320km) miles each day, or a mean speed of around 8 miles an
hour (13kph) over the whole distance. This would be a reasonable
rate of progress for such a train. British troop trains aimed to carry
a battalion (normally 1,000 men) and all its kit in two trains, with
a target track speed of 25mph (40 kph). (The French adopted a
different approach, using one large train, travelling at half that
speed.) We know from the war diary that the battalion was split
between two trains. A steady speed of 25 miles an hour would,
with a few lengthy stops, translate with little difficulty to a 12mph
average, close enough to the battalion's average speed over the
whole journey. It seems ironic that they should have taken, for part
of the journey, what would become a route of the French TGV,
which currently boasts average speeds of 175mph (280kph).

What a journey it must have been for those men. Travelling
down the beautiful Rhône Valley and along the Côte d'Azur
through Cannes and Nice must have been a whole new adventure,
offering unbelievable scenery and a vastly different climate. Not
surprisingly, 'the men were interested throughout the journey'!
'Halts repas' is a misspelling of the French haltes repas, which

literally translates as 'meal stops'. Morale would have been given a boost by the local support as they travelled. (Leaving the horrors of Flanders would have already given it a significant boost. Surely the new front couldn't be as terrible as the Ypres Salient?) The train would steam for a few hours, occasionally stopping, starting again, repeated day after day. It would not have been an especially comfortable journey, and slow even by the standards of troop trains, but it was an improvement on the soldiers' way of life in Flanders, as well as a break from the demanding activities at the front or in the training areas. The men might have had an idea of where and what they were heading for, but there was no great tradition in the British Army of keeping the troops informed about anything.

During one of the breaks in the journey, the troops must have been given the opportunity to buy from local shops. Harry bought a postcard and, on arrival at the end of the rail journey, was able to write a short note to Jack. Tortona, pictured on the card, is around a hundred miles (160km) short of Mantua and their journey's end.

Harry's postcard to Jack, bought in Tortona and sent when the battalion reached its destination.

Tortona - Ruderi dell'antico forte S. Vittorio

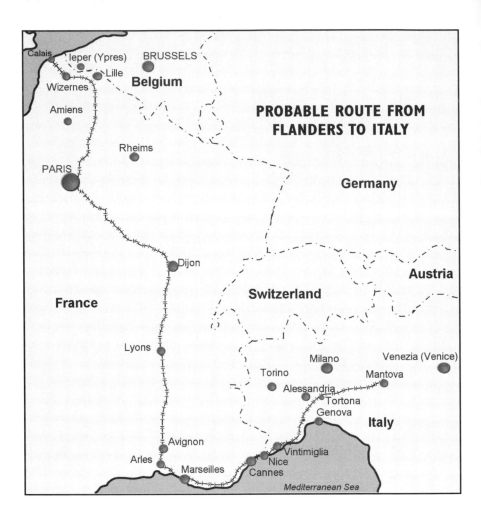

Nov 15th 1917

    Dear Jack

I am going on all right, will write as soon as possible. Hope the wedding [Jack's to Agnes; see Chapter 1] *comes off alright. Write and tell Ethel you have heard from me.*

    Love Harry

Having arrived in Italy, the division started on the long march to the front line, beginning, for Harry's battalion, with a short march to new billets at Ceresa. Things had grown a good deal more comfortable, as the war diary reports, rather less tersely than usual:

16 to 18 [November] *Billeted in good billets at CERESA, where satisfactory training was carried out. On the 18th a church parade was held. Whilst in the area the condition of the men was good, although the sick parades were a little larger than usual several men suffering with boils.*

19 The Division commenced its march forward to concentration area. The BN moved off at 8.30 am by march route to SUSANO CORTA CHIAVICHE (about 12 miles [20km]) arriving in Billets at 3.30 pm. The marching was good, no men falling out.

20 The march was resumed at 7 am to NIGARA (8 miles [13km]) the Bn in Billets by 11am. The high standard of marching was still maintained and very few men had blistered feet.

21 Bn moved off at 6.30 am to LENAGO (12 miles [20km]), arriving in Billets at 3 pm. The marching was again good, and the transport was very clean & smart.

22 Bn moved off at 7 am to Noventa (16 miles [26km]) arriving in Billets at 1430 pm. The men marched very well and not a man fell out. Several men's feet were blistered.

23 The march was resumed at 9 am to PONT du BARBARANO (7 miles [11km]) and the Bn was in Billets by 1 pm.

Because the distance marched on the 23rd was one of the shorter ones, and the men were in billets by lunchtime, Harry had the chance to write a short letter home.

Nov 23rd 1917

Dear Kate.

Just a line to let you know I'm going on all right. I should be pleased if you could send some powder the next time you write the cake was grand you sent. I hope you get on all right with your fresh job. my address is the same only put Italy instead of France. Would be pleased if you could write once a week if it was only a line will write again as soon as possible.

With best love

Harry

Then they were off again, the war diary still solemnly recording the distances marched each day:

24 At 7 am the Bn moved off to ST MARIA (10 miles [16km]), arriving there at 1 pm.

25 Moved off at 7am to ISOLA di CARTURO (6¹/2 miles [10km]) and in Billets by 11 am. During the last three days the march discipline was still very good, and no men fell out. The men were in good condition and their feet were sound.

The march having ended in the morning, Harry was able to write another letter:

25 November 1917

> Dear Jack
>
> I hope you are getting on alright as I am in good health at present except bad feet after a lot of marching. My address is the same as usual, except you must put Italy instead of France. When you write I should be glad if you would send an envelope and paper. I have had no white bread lately we have been on Italian rashing [rations] would be glad if you could send me a parcel I have not had any for weeks. Let me know how you are getting on. I think Mr. Thomas's son is in the same division as we are. if so he has come to Italy too. I shall be glad to get home again to see you all. Willie is getting on well and gets a big boy they are all in good health and dad is about the same. I think he is a marvellous fellow. We have seen some fine scenery on our travels. We were 4 or 5 days in the train it is alright down south of France and very pretty. Write as soon as possible
>
> with best love
>
> Harry

And still the battalion marched:

26 & 27 inspections were held on the 26th & training resumed the following day. The sick parades were large, the chief complaint being blistered feet, but the rest benefitted the men greatly.

28 The march resumed at 8am to ISOLA ROMOLO (12 miles [20km]), the Bn arriving in Billets by 4pm.

29 At 9am Bn moved off to SONTREIA (7 miles [11km]) and were in Billets by 12 noon. The march discipline throughout the march

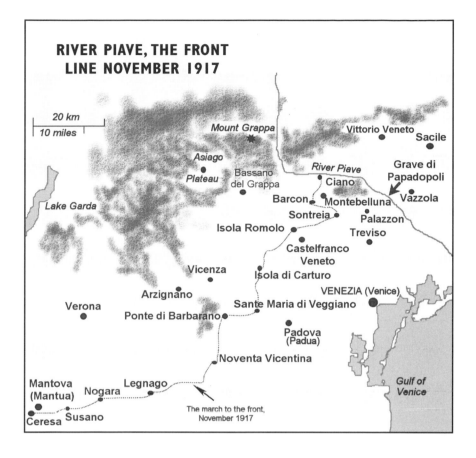

RIVER PIAVE, THE FRONT LINE NOVEMBER 1917

20 km
10 miles

Mount Grappa
Vittorio Veneto
Sacile
Asiago Plateau
Bassano del Grappa
River Piave
Ciano
Grave di Papadopoli
Lake Garda
Barcon
Montebelluna
Vazzola
Sontreia
Palazzon
Isola Romolo
Treviso
Castelfranco Veneto
Vicenza
Isola di Carturo
VENEZIA (Venice)
Arzignano
Sante Maria di Veggiano
Verona
Ponte di Barbarano
Padova (Padua)
Noventa Vicentina
Gulf of Venice
Mantova (Mantua)
Nogara
Legnago
Ceresa
Susano
The march to the front, November 1917

was excellent, and very few men were carried on the Ambulance – no men fell out throughout the march.

30 Bn in Billets - the C.O. inspected Companies in Drill order and was satisfied with the smart appearance of the Bn. The majority of the men were bathed.

This was an army moving on foot in 1917. The heavy equipment would be transported by horse-drawn general-service wagon and motor lorry. The men would march as a body, generally in companies, carrying their full military equipment. Day after day the condition of feet, particularly, would deteriorate through ill-fitting boots and poor-quality, badly (and rarely) washed socks.

Harry had been marching for over a week when he asked Kate for powder, presumably talcum powder for his feet, and to ease chafing where his uniform rubbed against his skin.

The total distance marched by the battalion was almost 110 miles (175km). The distances don't sound too demanding in today's terms, but with few exceptions the men would have been carrying their normal equipment and rifles, all of which would weigh up to 65 pounds (30kg). On top of this, they were not well fed and had just spent six months in the Flanders sector of the Western Front. Nor was their kit and equipment ideal for long-distance marching, and they would have suffered much chafing, blistering and general discomfort. Even so, it was still a considerable improvement over life in the trenches around Ypres.

They were not to be in Sontreia for long, but while there continued with training, and drill also made a no doubt unwelcome reappearance:

1st [December] *battalion in billets at SONTREIA. Company training in Running Drill, Musketry: Bayonet fighting, Arms Drill and Company Drill was continued with.*

Harry found time to write to Jack on the same day:

Dec 1st 1917

Dear Jack

I have just received a small packet from you and was very pleased with it. It was a good job it was something that would keep as it was dated Nov 8th. I have also received a letter Nov 14th. The lady you are marrying I can remember quite well. Well I hope you are married by now. I can remember two lady teachers Miss James and a Miss Meredith who were at East Oxford. We have had some good marches this last fortnight which I should have enjoyed better had we not quite so much to carry. The weather has been just right for marching the roads are very level out here you can see all the big hills or mountains in the distance with snow on them the scenery would be grand in summer time. I am pleased they are going on all right at home and

that you are keeping well. glad to hear about Kate. I think it is very
good of them to buy you a present worth about £10 it should be a
good one. We are getting on better for food now but very short of bread.
Don't forget to put Italy instead of France I hope you have a Merry
xmas and a Happy new year. I'm going to try to get a card to send
you for Christmas. Write back as soon as you can and don't forget.

Yours Harry

A wedding present costing £10 is remarkably generous. At today's values £10 in 1917 would be worth well over £500. Yet the only member of the family earning a regular wage would seem to be Kate (Jack would have been paid a stipend by the Church). I would love to know what they actually spent the money on, and who contributed, but, sadly, the details have long since been forgotten.

On the following day, the 9th York and Lancasters completed their journey: '2nd [December] Battalion moved off at 11 A.M. and marched to billets at BARCON arriving there at 2.40 P.M.' This was a decent march of around eight miles (13km), and was followed by a seven-mile march to the front line on the River Piave.

It had taken just over three weeks to relocate the 23rd Division more than a thousand miles to another country, a fresh climate and, as we shall see, to a very different fighting environment.

CHAPTER 8

THE PIAVE RIVER DEFENCE LINE

ON 5 DECEMBER 1917 the 9th Battalion, York and Lancaster Regiment took its place supporting the front line that followed the southern bank of the Piave River. The river rises in the Dolomites and flows south-south-west before turning south-eastwards to flow into the Gulf of Venice some twenty miles north-east of that city. It was along this roughly west-to-east length of the river that the Austro-Hungarian advance following the Italian rout at Caporetto was finally halted. The countryside, to Harry and his comrades, would be very different from the area around Ypres, with much green vegetation and magnificent views. To the south-east, Venice and the Adriatic Sea were less than thirty miles away; to the north, the foothills of the Dolomite Mountains would be clearly visible.

The next four months were spent on the Piave front, supporting the defensive effort. Most of the time was spent in the vicinity of Montebelluna, about twelve miles (20km) north-east of Treviso at the foot of the Montella high ground, towards the centre of the plain and twenty-five miles (40km) or so due north of Venice. In the middle of February there was two-day march to a new location, still on the Piave front, but much closer to the mountains. After nine days there, during which scouts from the battalion actually climbed the nearby mountain, they set off and marched the twenty-five miles (40km) back to Montebelluna. In the Second World War this would have been viewed as a typical army SNAFU (Situation Normal, All Fouled Up – the polite version).

The Piave was very different from rivers the British soldiers would have known or seen before. Once the body of water reached the Venetian Plain, where it turns eastwards through 90 degrees to head for the Adriatic, the river split into many small channels and broadened to a width of several hundred yards. This had a considerable effect on the positions of the opposing armies. In Flanders, the enemy lines were directly ahead, within easy range of a rifle shot, and sometimes only tens of yards away. Here, the river provided a secure boundary that pushed the enemy away to a relatively remote distance. As a result, defensive arrangements differed radically from those on the Western Front. Any patrolling, the placing of wire entanglements, the siting of gun lines, even trench design, all needed to be modified to suit new conditions.

In 1918 the river was a much more impressive feature than is the case today. The channels were much deeper then, and there was a greater head of water. Irrigation, industry and modern demands for water have reduced the amount of water reaching the plain.

By 12 November the Italian Army had successfully halted the rapid advance of the Austro-Hungarians in fighting which, as part of the Battle of Caporetto, is often known as the First Battle of the Piave. (It is possible, however, that the Austro-Hungarians had set the Piave as an objective, and had decided to halt the offensive there before their lines of communication became dangerously stretched.) The arrival of British and French reinforcements, all tried and tested on the Western Front, effectively locked the opposing forces into these positions.

This section of Harry's war is difficult to describe, for by early December the Italian theatre of war was quite static on the Piave. The war diary account shows, however, that it was not without its dangers:

> *3rd* [December] *The 70th Brigade* [which included the 9th York and Lancasters] *relieved the 136th Regt of the 70th Italian Division in the left sub-section. (MONTELLO SECTOR). The Battalion moved off at 9.45 A.M. and marched to CIANO where it relieved the 1st Battalion 136th Italian Regt; and became support Battalion. After one hours marching the Battn halted and dinners and teas were served in a field. Sports were held in the afternoon. The march was resumed about 4.0 P.M. to CIANO. Relief complete about 8.0 P.M.*

(This day's account seems almost bizarre. The battalion is to march to the front line but, on the way, stops for a picnic and sports. Presumably there was a good reason, but the military mind has not always been easy to understand.)

4th, 5th, 6th [December] *Battalion in Support in CIANO.*
7th 'A', 'B' and 'D' Coys and Battalion [HQ?] *moved to new billets.*
8th, 9th 10th Battalion in support. Whilst in support Companies worked on defences, and improved sanitary conditions etc. and made hurdles [rectangular sections of fencing made by interweaving flexible branches on a wooden frame; used to shore up trenches, or possibly as screens against enemy sniper fire].
11th Battalion should have been relieved by the 8th York & Lancasters, but owing to continuous shelling of our front during the day and the change in the weather, the Brigade Commander cancelled relief. Warning Order received in the early hours to the effect that Austrians were massing, the Battn 'stood to'. Casualties: 6 O.R.'s wounded.
12th Battalion relieved the 8th K.O.Y.L.I. and became the Left front line Battalion of the Left Brigade. Relief complete at 7.30 P.M. Dispositions were as follows;- A Company Left Front Company. 'D' Company, Centre Front Company. 'B' Company Right Front Company. 'C' Company [Harry's] *Support Company. Courts Martial Promulgated on: No. 16968 Sgt McGowan J, and No. 16210 Sgt Boyes J W.*
13th–19th Battalion in new dispositions. Draft of 98 O.R.s joined at transport lines on 14th inst. 2nd Lt Park M.C. and 2nd Lt Lewis joined on the 14th inst. Whilst in the line, the defence scheme was prepared. Line patrols were out nightly along the PIAVE river bed. Brigade was relieved by 68th Brigade [also of 23rd division].

Two weeks in, or close to, the front line is quite a lengthy tour. Almost certainly, the conditions were better than at Ypres, and the men were well rested and, for the main part, were in support of the front-line units. A considerable part of the battalion's efforts was directed towards stabilizing and improving the trench environment, bringing it to an acceptable standard for these experienced soldiers.

Yet there was some significant action, with shelling and a potential attack, the battalion suffering some casualties. The Piave front may well have been different to Flanders, but it was still a dangerous place to be. On the plains, where the battalion is at this time, the weather would be reasonably good, although the mountains a few miles to the north would be snow-capped by mid-December.

As normal, once out of the line, all equipment is to be cleaned and checked.

20th [December] *In billets at MONTEBELLUNA.*
Rifle, Bayonet, SAA, Clothing, equipment, box respirators, P.H. Helmet, iron rations [tinned, dried or non-perishable rations issued to soldiers for use when cut off from regular supplies] *and Field dressings inspections. C. O. inspected N. C. O's of battalions under C. S.'s M.* [company sergeant-majors; the war diary is here referring to them as 'company sergeants-major']. *Specialists trained under their own officers.*

Christmas Day, spent at Montebelluna, brought a few comforts, spiritual and regimental as well as personal.

December 25th Church Service in the morning.
First Round (Match 'B' of the Brigade Football Competition was played between:– 9th Y & L & Brigade Head Quarters and 70th Light Trench Mortar Battery. Kick off 10.30 A.M. Result 9th Y & L, 7 goals. Brigade Head Quarters etc. 1.
The men had their Christmas dinner in their billets which consisted of roast pork, Christmas pudding, fruit and wine.
The Battalion had a concert in the Medical School in MONTEBELLUNA in the evening.

The embroidered Christmas card Harry received from his wife, Ethel, shown above, is a wonder. It somehow survived and came home safely with him.

WITH THE
BEST OF GOOD WISHES,
Not only for
Christmas and the New Year,
But for all times

From *Harry*

The regiment itself even provided Christmas cards for the officers and men to send home. The one shown above is in very good condition and is probably the card Harry sent to Jack, mentioned in his letter of 30 December. By Boxing Day, however, the battalion was back at work, as assiduously recorded in the war diary:

26th [December] *Battalion training as follows, Close Order Drill, Saluting Drill, Extended Order Drill. Guard Duties and Lectures. The Following Classes assembled at the Brigade School:- Signalling Class 10 O.R.'s. Lewis Gun Class N.C.O. and six men. General Class 20 untrained men* [from the draft of 13 December]. *In the evening hostile aeroplanes bombed MONTEBELLUNA but caused no casualties in the Battalion.*

I still find it hard to believe that drill and saluting should form such an important part of training when these men may at any time be involved in dangerous activities in the front line. The football is looking promising, however. That does seem at least a reasonable activity for the men as a diversion from the deadly serious business of war.

28th [December] *– All Companies range practices. Revolver practice for all officers. Specialists under their own officers.*

'C' Match of the 2nd round of the Brigade Football Competition was played between:–

9th Y & L v 70th Machine Gun Coy Kick off 2.30 P.M.

Result 9th Y & L three goals – 70th Machine Gun Coy one goal.

On the 30th, Harry was able to write two very optimistic letters home. Already, we can sense that the Italian experience is infinitely preferable to what he had undergone on the Western Front. Food parcels are, as always, an important topic in his letters.

> *30/12/1917*
> *32507 9th Batt York and Lancs, C Company,*
> *12 platoon L. G. section, BEF Italy*

Dear Jack

I have received a letter from you and a box of biscuits all right. I got them on Christmas morning and you can bet how pleased I was. I have also had a letter from Kate she said she was having a holiday this Christmas the first for seven years. I hope she enjoys herself. I'm sorry to hear that Mr. Thomas's son as got killed what date did it happen. I have had a letter from Mrs. Higgins I shall write back as soon as possible. Ethel says Connie has not been very well lately but I hope she gets on alright. I am pleased to here you are getting on all right and very happy. I hope you enjoyed yourself this Christmas. They all seem to be well again at home except Connie and I think she will be alright. Glad you liked the [Christmas] card I sent you. I thought it would suit alright. It is very cold out here at night but it is alright at daytime. Write back as soon as you can and let me know how you are getting on.

With best love from
Harry

He manages not to write quite the same things in his letter to Kate, although food parcels again figure, as does his anxiety about Connie's health. Presumably Kate, as Connie's natural mother, would have kept a very close, if discreet, watch over her daughter.

December 30 1917

32507 9th Batt York and Lancs, C Company

12 platoon L. G. section, BEF Italy

Dear Kate

I have received a letter from you and was very pleased, it is such a long time since I had one. I have not received the parcel yet and I hope it will come I am ready for it I think parcels will reach us all right after Christmas. It is very cold at night but in the daytime it is alright. I hope you got home for Christmas and found them well and enjoyed your holiday. Did you get the card I sent you. I have had a letter from Jack he's getting on alright, I am pleased to hear it. I hope Connie is better when you receive this letter. Let me know how Willie is if you happen to get home. Has Annie been to see Jack since he got married. Ethel said she was very likely going after Christmas. Glad you are getting on alright at Leeds but I did not expect you would like it the same as London. I hope you have had a Merry Christmas and Happy New Year. Write back as soon as possible and let me know how you are all going on.

With love from Harry

The new year finds the battalion still drilling:

2nd [January] *Montebelluna. Physical Drill. Saluting Drill. Box Respirator Drill and musketry. The working parties supplied were: 1 officer, 25 men for D.G.O. Montebelluna. 1 officer and 30 men at MONTEBELLUNA station unloading flax. 1 N.C.O. and 20 men under O.C. Sanitary Section, MONTEBELLUNA. Loading party of 1 sergeant and 10 O.R. to report to 128 Fld Co Corps R.E. Dump* [i.e. to a Field Company of the Royal Engineers at the ammunition dump for the entire corps]. *The Armourer Sergeant inspected rifles of Companies. Bgde Football Championship Final. 8th Y & L v 9th Y & L .*

Result 9th 2 8th 0

Baths. Lecture by G.S.O. [i.e. a general staff officer] *of the Division, in Bgde Recreation Room BIADENE. All Platoon Comders. attended. Identification Cards issued to all officers.*

More saluting . . . It just seems so good that Harry's battalion has won the football final. It must have been a morale booster for the men (although Harry never mentions football in his letters). I am not sure of the military function, if any, of the flax that was unloaded; the working party may have been detailed to empty a train so that it could be used for a military purpose.

The war diary entry for the following week confirms that the Piave here followed several channels:

5th–12th [January] *Bn in the line. During this period in spite of snow and exceptionally cold weather several attempts were made by patrols to cross the river and to reach the enemy's line but owing to the swiftness of the stream its depth and the lack of any chart, no crossing could be effected for some time. Towards the end of our tour in the front line however 2/Lt Flory with a patrol succeeded in definitely locating a sufficiently shallow spot in each stream to enable a continuous crossing to be made and this route has been definitely established. On the first occasion of a patrol crossing the entire bed of the river it was heavily fired upon by a post and withdrew but this post as was ascertained later was removed to a position further East.*

We can see how things are quite different on this front. By now the cold weather would be spilling down from the mountains. Patrols would have to deal with a river in the way, rather than, as in the Ypres sector, the barbed-wire entanglements and shell holes of no man's land. Defensive measures would be rather different, too. In Flanders, gaps in the wire necessary to allow patrols and even attacking troops a way forward through the entanglements would be targeted. Here the focus would be on the shallow river crossings as possible danger spots.

For his part, Harry takes advantage of the relative quietness of this sector to write home again (Bonser was Harry's mother's maiden name, so Shelton and Jack must almost certainly be an uncle and a cousin, respectively):

Jan 9th/1917
32507/9th York & Lancs Batt, C. Company,

12 Platoon L.G.S., B.E.F. Italy

Dear Kate

I have just received your parcel alright everything was in good order. I am glad you are going on alright and like your job. How did you go on at Christmas. Ethel tells me you managed to get home for a week. How did you find Connie and Willie where they alright, well how did you find them all. I hope you enjoyed yourself. I am going to write home. It is very cold out here at night but we have some nice days. I am sorry to hear about Uncle Shelton and about Jack Bonser getting wounded. I hope he gets on alright. Write as often as you can. I think we shall get our letters alright now. I shall be glad to see you all again.

With love
from Harry

A few days later:

Jan 14 1918

32507 / 9th Batt York and Lancs , C Company,

12 platoon L. G. S., BEF Italy

Dear Jack

I have received your letter. I have also received two parcels of woollen goods from Mrs. Higgins but you can't carry a lot of stuff about we have enough to carry about. It was very good, their was a nice jersey home made which I am keeping and some socks so I had a clean and new rig out which I wanted. Your biscuits was grand and I enjoyed them. I have also had a nice parcel from Kate she said she enjoyed the Christmas alright at home. Willie and Connie as not been very well but they are going on alright now. Kate says Willie gets a rum little chap and can say anything. I am pleased to hear you are going on alright and that you are very comfortable and settled down. It is still very cold out here at night and we have had some snow. it is different to being out in France [in fact, Belgium], *very quiet. Write and let me know how you're getting on as soon as possible. As Kate or Annie been to see you yet. I have wrote to Mrs. Higgins so I shall no doubt have a letter from either Mrs. Higgins or Miss Worthington. Pleased you liked the card. With best love*

Harry

In that war, the soldiers of the British infantry carried everything they owned, as well as everything with which they had officially been issued (and for which they were personally accountable). As attractive as extra clothing must have seemed, the penalty was that it would have to be carried. Harry is sensibly selective in what he holds on to. Food is not a problem as it can soon be shared out and eaten. Clothes are a little more difficult. Within the restrictions of the regulations about uniform, the soldiers would wear anything that made them more comfortable. It wasn't always possible to exchange torn or worn-through articles of uniform or issue clothing in the line, so they just had to improvise or 'lump it'. As to the rest of the letter, I'm afraid that I know nothing of

Mrs Higgins or Miss Worthington, but it is likely that they were either neighbours or family friends.

> *21st–31st* [January] *Bn in the line. This period has been distinguished for the great deal of work done in the connection with the improvement and strengthening of our trenches and dug outs also for the nightly patrols. Officers & men have been continuously practised in patrol*[ing] *the river bed at night and the negotiable spots of the various streams have been pointed out to each officer and man. Enemy posts have been engaged but we have suffered no casualties up to date. A miniature range has been built and every man has been trained and practised with the rifle whilst the promotion of Inter Company and Inter Platoon* [shooting] *Competitions has* [sic] *interested and encouraged the men tremendously.*

MENTIONED IN DISPATCHES
(London Gazette Supplement, December 21st 1917)
Lt Col. D. Rumbold D.S.O. M.C.
Major D. Lewis M.C.
Major F. Colley D.S.O. and bar
Capt. R. J. M. Leakey
Capt. N. Macleod
Capt. L. Tester
No 15394 – CSM [company sergeant-major] *Oldfield*

The defences occupied by the battalion needed continual attention, to get them, and then to keep them up to the standard that they were used to in Flanders. As the war diary mentions, all the likely pitfalls or advantages that might be of use in an assault have been scouted and then pointed out to everyone, signifying a really competent approach by the battalion. (A mention in dispatches indicates that an officer, warrant officer, NCO or other rank has been singled out by name in the official dispatch of a senior commander, usually the army commander, in the relevant sector of the front. It is indicated by a small bronze oak leaf worn on the ribbon of the medal awarded for that particular campaign; the recipient also gets a certificate.)

Harry's next letter, to Jack, is undeniably a curiosity:

Jan 29/1/18
32507/9th Batt Y &L, C Company,
12 Platoon L.G.S., IEF

Dear Jack

I have received your long letter and tin of salmon which was very good.
I was sorry to hear the bad news about Uncle [Shelton] and Jack
Bonser. I did not know he was died but I heard he was wounded very
bad. I was glad . . . [turn page] . . . to hear that you and Kate went
to the funeral it was the least you could do. I am also pleased Mrs.
Higgins liked the letter which I wrote. We are on that part of the line
you seen in the paper and it is quite true except for the long march
after but they left the rum bottle out which they never forget to take
. . . [turn page] . . . Their is five or six parts [i.e. channels] of the
river they have to cross before they get to the other side it is very wide
and the farthest away from the enemy I have been when in the front
line. I have not had the job yet but might get it any time a fighting
patrol mostly as a lewis gun and three or four of the team . . . [turn
page] . . . with them our batt as had no luck yet, mostly get spotted.
I was pleased you found Willie and Connie alright, but we can except
[expect?] dad being bad I think he has been very lucky I hope he gets
better. I hope the war is finished before you have to come out their are
plenty of younger men [Jack is forty-nine].

Write as soon as possible.
With Love from
Harry

This is a strange letter, for it doesn't quite make sense. I have
indicated the ends of pages so that readers can form their own
judgements about it. I wonder whether there's a page missing, or
whether 'they left the rum bottle out which they never forget
to take' may be significant. If so, its finders were battle-hardened
soldiers, and I can imagine that coming across a gallon of strong
rum lying unattended would not have caused a lot of earnest
discussion among them. Nor would they have been much worried

by such trivial matters as the likely consequences. At all events, I hope that Harry and his pals did actually enjoy a few mugs of rum. It may be that he then tried to write a letter . . .

According to the battalion's war diary, Harry was in the front line when he wrote this letter. It was not without its dangers, but it would have been quieter than the front line in Flanders. And for all that the letter rambles in places, it contains a very clear description of the River Piave, as well as an indication of what the troops faced in the forward trenches.

(Note for the enthusiast. 'BEF Italy' [British Expeditionary Force – Italy] has just changed to 'IEF' [Italian Expeditionary Force]. I gather that this was an official change to reflect the involvement of the other Allied forces.)

1st [February] *Battn in the line. Left Bn* [of the] *Right Brigade Disposition:*
B Coy Right Front Line Coy, C Centre
D Left
A Support Coy
2nd & 3rd In the line. All works, competitions and general cleaning up referred to in final part of January diary maintained with unabated energy until relieved by the 11th NORTHUMBERLAND FUSILIERS on the evening of 3rd. Platoons moved independently by route CIANO – BUSCO thence to billets in BIADENE. Bn in billets at 11 p.m.

As readers have probably come to expect by now, Harry used the time out of the line to write to both Kate and Jack.

Feb 7th /1918
32507/ 9th Batt York & Lanc Regt., C Company,
12 Platoon L.G.S., I.E.F.
P.S. (Put I.E.F. on address and leave Italy out)
Dear Kate
I have received your letter. I also received your parcel. it was in good order. The weather here is very cold at night, but it is quite warm in the day. I have received a letter from Jack he's going on alright and said they

were alright at Ilkeston [i.e. Harry's wife and his children] *excepting dad who does not seem to get much better. I was sorry to here the bad news I got about Jack Bonser and Uncle.* [Harry's brother] *Jack's wife was headmistress at East Oxford Girls school and also head mistress of the Girls Night School. of course that is some years back. I don't know how long she remained there, but I remember her quite well. He often sends me bits of things which come in very useful. I don't know whether I told you that I had a parcel from Mrs. Higgins at Christmas. I don't know when I shall get a leave I don't suppose it will be just yet as there is plenty to go before me, but anyhow I would certainly let you know. Ethel tells me what a job it is to get a bit of butter, tea or sugar [food rationing had finally been introduced in Britain in January, largely in response to the German U-boat campaign against Allied shipping]. I hope you're keeping in good health as I am very well at the present. Write back as often as you can and I will answer as many as possible.*

With best love from Harry

Feb 7th / 1918

32507/ 9th Batt York & Lanc Regt., C Company,

12 Platoon L.G.S., I.E.F.

P.S. (Put I.E.F. on address and leave Italy out)

Dear Jack

I have received your letter and I also got your small parcel alright. I was very pleased to hear that you are both keeping well and hope you remain so. The news was very sad which I have had about Jack Bonser and Uncle what had Aunt Annie got to say I don't suppose she would stay very long especially were Aunt Polly was. I shall never forget her tongue. It does not seem that she has altered much. It must have upset Uncle a great deal when he heard about Jack's death and no doubt it would make him worse. The weather here is still very cold at night but it is grand in the day. I don't suppose the war will be over just yet it looks like lasting another twelve months to me, I hope I'm wrong. I think America has got to have a good try at it before it finishes. Things look very bad in England as regards food they seem short all over of course we get our usual rations which is none to big, but we cant grumble we have missed something coming out here and leaving Flanders I hope we don't go back again, things are very quiet out here, well they have been

up to now but we don't know how long they going to last. When in the
front line we have had a fire at night and sometimes we have been in
an old house so you can bet we are not bothered much by shells. I could
not say where the H.A.C. [Honourable Artillery Company] is. It
is a London Regt. I remember quite well when we were going in the
trenches at Ypres they were just being releived. I got lost I could not get
along it was up to the waist in slug [sludge?] and water. I came across
some chaps who are also lost and they said they belong to the H.A.C.
It is supposed to be a Toffs regt. Artillery is only a name they have given
them they belong to the infantry. I don't know how they went on but
I found my way after wandering about for two or three hours. I shall
never forget the times we had up there. I don't know how we managed
sometimes, but I don't feel no worse for it now, but I hope that we don't
get anything like it again. We have to get our feet rubbed every morning
with whale oil when in the trenches every morning it is cold at night.

Write back as soon as possible
With best love to you both
Harry

This wonderful letter from Harry to Jack gives us, for once, a
great deal of information. He introduces some new characters
that I know nothing about – since there is no one left alive to
ask, readers will have to draw their own conclusions. Aunt Polly
sounds like a dragon, but who knows? Aunt Annie is unlikely to
be Harry's sister, Sarah Anne, although she was always known
as Annie. As mentioned, Jack Bonser would have been Harry's
cousin or another quite close relation. He seems to have died
from wounds, and his death to have had a profound effect upon
'Uncle Shelton', who is possibly his father.

The sentence 'I don't suppose the war will be over just yet...'
was picked up from the blog and, with a picture of Harry, used on
a set of postage stamps for the British Indian Ocean Territories
commemorating the ninetieth anniversary of the end of the war.

The front line sounds bearable, certainly in comparison to
the Ypres Salient. A fire on the cold nights would have been a
luxury; in Flanders, however, a fire, or anything that gave away

the presence of troops, such as the flare of a match to light a cigarette, would have immediately attracted a lethal attack from rifles, machine guns, shells or trench mortars – or all of them.

We then come to Harry's best description of Flanders, written months after he left that theatre of operations. Perhaps he feels more comfortable describing it now he's no longer there. The HAC he mentions (Jack has obviously asked him about it) is the Honourable Artillery Company, then, as now, a London-based Reserve unit which, despite its name, raised a number of infantry battalions during the Great War, as well as fielding artillery batteries. The horror of being lost in waist-deep 'slug' can only be imagined. Harry's hope that 'we don't get anything like it again' shows how much better the conditions are in Italy.

Trench foot was a serious problem among the troops and was addressed with regular inspections and the daily application of whale oil. In the muddy conditions of Flanders, and elsewhere, soldiers would be, understandably, reluctant to remove their boots and socks for the duration of a tour in the trenches which might be for up to two weeks. For that period, their feet would be constantly cold, dirty and wet, and liable to develop an infection that would, literally, rot the feet. Severe cases could lead to amputation or even death. Until the policy of inspecting and oiling the feet was adopted, the ailment had been a significant problem in the trench-bound armies.

Meanwhile the battalion continues to train – and to drill…

14th [February] *Divl. Rifle Range allotted to the Batn. Practices in the musketry course part 1 continued. Remainder of the morning Coys at disposal of Os. C. Coys for Arms Drill, Saluting Drill and Platoon Drill. Lewis Gunners into Coys for range practice, arms drill etc. Signallers and Scouts under their respective officers. In the afternoon one good instructor and twelve men per Coy. (worst shots) reported to the Miniature* [i.e. 25-yard] *Range under L.G.O.* [Lewis gun officer]. *The 3rd re-play for the Divl. Championship between 69th & 70th Brigade took place on the Divl. Football Ground MONTEBELLUNA, resulting in a victory for the 70th Brigade. Score 70th 3 goals 69th 1 goal. 10*

N.C.O.s previously detailed, reported with 2nd/Lt W DARRELL
to the 128th Field Coy R.E. for instruction in knotting and lashing.
On the evenings of the 12th and 13th of this month, a party of artistes
styling themselves 'THE TIMIDS' gave two excellent performances in
the large hall of the Hd. Qrs Billet. The troop [troupe] was entirely
composed of members of the 70th Field Ambulance.

The 9th Battalion, York and Lancaster Regiment was part of
70 Brigade which, with 68 and 69 Brigades, made up the 23rd
Division, itself part of the Second Army.

16th [February] Battn. marched to LORIA and took over billets from
the 12th Battn EAST SURREY Regt. Battn. moved off at 8.30
am. Route Posmo[?] – C. MORA – BUSTA. Dinners on arrival in
Billets. Battn. in billets at 2 pm.
17th Battn. moved to VILLA FIETTA near CRESPANO. Taking
over billets from the 19th Battn. Middlesex Regt. (Pioneers) Dinners
on arrival in billets. Battn. in billets at 3pm.
18th Coys at Os. C. Coys' disposal for inspection & thorough
cleaning of billets and equipment. Signallers under their own officer.
The Scouts under the Scout Officer climbed Mount GRAPPA where
a detachment of Italians (65th Div) made them welcome and gave
them a loaf of bread each!

During the rest of February and into early March, Harry was able
to write several letters, while the battalion remained in billets and
continued with training.

Feb 18th/1918
32507/9th Batt York & Lancs., C Company,
12 Platoon L.G.S., I.E.F.

Dear Jack
I am pleased to hear that you are both getting on well. the weather here
is still very cold. we are very near the mountains now. I expect we shall
get it hot when the weather does change. I should not be surprised if
we don't have another move before long. I have been alright in Italy
up to now. I hope to remain so. We cannot grumble at the quiet time

we have had. Glad to hear that they are going on alright at Ilkeston. I think they would have been to see you only the train fare is such a lot of money. I was very pleased with the two papers you sent it was just what I wanted. there is some grand scenery round here it would be alright for a holiday in peace time, but I dont know when that will be. I hope it will not be long as I am ready to get back any time. What had Aunt annie to say did she stay long at Uncle Shelton's it was a very sad affair and I was very sorry. It will soon be Willie birthday again in March. but I dont suppose I shall be able to send anything as there is not much to get here. Write as often as you can.

  With best Love to you both
  Harry

Feb 22/2/18
32509/ 9th Batt, York & Lancs Regt., C Company,
12 Platoon L.G.S., I.E.F.

  Dear Kate,
I have received your parcel alright and it is very good. I have had a letter from Jack and one from Ethel I was pleased to hear that they are going on alright and that Jack is quite happy in his married life. Ethel tells me what a rum chap Willie gets and is a very good talker. he can say anything. I should very much like to see him and Connie. They tell me that dad does not get much better but he is getting an old man. I think he will be better as the weather gets warmer, well I hope so. Write back as often as you can and let me know how you are getting on.

  With best Love
  Harry

Harry's father would have been seventy-three years old at the time – certainly a good age in 1918.

Feb 22/2/18
32509/ 9th Batt., York & Lancs Regt., C Company,
12 Platoon, L.G.S.

  Dear Jack
I received your letter yesterday and was very pleased with it. The salmon was alright and tasted a treat. I have seen nothing of the Batt you spoke of out hear, you ask me in your letter last time. I was

pleased to hear that they were going on alright a [at] *Ilkeston and in good health. I am also feeling well myself. I am glad that you are getting on alright and I wish to be remembered to your wife. Ethel tells me that Willie was quite willing to go back with you last time you went home. he must be a rum chap. Kate as just sent me a cake so I am alright.*

With best love to you both Write back as soon as possible.

Harry.

A cake, tinned salmon – everything was indeed 'alright'. The war diary, however, is still concerned with training, and especially musketry:

28th [February] *'B' and C Coys training in hill fighting on the MONTELLO. 'A' and 'D' Coys at Os. C. Coys disposal for Company training. Field Firing Range allotted to 'A' and 'D' Coys from noon to dusk. Specialists under their own Officers. During the month a marked improvement has taken place in the men's shooting.*

In his next letter Harry, rather touchingly, commiserates with civilians at home now enduring food rationing:

March 3rd/1918

32507/9 Batt York & Lancs Regt., C. Company,

12 Platoon L G S., I.E.F

Dear Kate

I am pleased you are getting on alright. I am in good health at present. I am glad they are keeping well at Ilkeston, it is Willie's Birthday this month. I hope the war will be over before it comes round again. It must be bad for you in England being so short of food it will be a good job when it is over. We are not so bad off for food out hear and cannot grumble, not in war time. I have had a letter from Jack he says that he and his wife are keeping well and that he will not be required for the army so he is alright, I am very pleased. Write as often as you can and let me know when you pay Jack a visit. The scenery here is alright we are quite close to the mountains and they look well. It takes five hours to get to the top of some and they are not the largest it would be alright out hear in peace time We can get plenty of fruit out here oranges and apples etc. but we dont get paid often enough. I think I must be a nice bit in credit.

With best love

Harry

(PS) Put I.E.F on letters not B.E.F.

Willie will be two on 23 March. A plentiful supply of fruit, especially oranges would have been an astonishing luxury for an East Midlands man. Harry must be describing the scouting expedition to the top of Mount Grappa, mentioned in the war diary entry for 18 February. It seems, too, that Jack has had confirmation that he won't be conscripted.

For this letter to Kate, Harry used a 'green envelope', which were issued only sparingly to soldiers and were much coveted. Instead of Battalion Headquarters reading and censoring a letter, the writer sealed it in one of these envelopes and signed the declaration on the front; it was then sent unread. The letter

A 'green envelope', showing the declaration that Harry signed.

might be checked by a censor away from the front, although probably only a small proportion were, which in turn meant that a soldier could write quite personal details without fear of local embarrassment.

Harry's next letter to Jack rehearses much of what he had written to Kate:

March 4th/1918

32507/9 Batt York and Lanc Regt., C. Company

12 Platoon L.G.S., I.E.F

Dear Jack

I have received your paper's and was very pleased with them I am glad that you are both keeping well. as I am alright at present. I am pleased to hear that you are able to stay at home and that the army will not require you. I have had a letter from Ethel and she says that dad does not get much better. I am glad that you have an idea where abouts I am things are still quite [quiet] I hope they remain so. We are not doing so bad for food out here it would be better if we got paid more regular we have only drawn ten lires in a month that is equal to five shillings [£0.25] in English money, so I think we shall have a bit to our credit, we get plenty of fruit out here oranges and apples etc. It will be Willie's birthday this month [23rd] but I shall not be able to send him anything. We see some fine scenery out here we are quite close to the mountains some of these take about five hours to climb and they are not the highest. it is different to flanders being out here. I think Kate will try to get a day or two off to see you she told me in her last letter that she would like to pay you a visit. Write back as soon as possible I am always glad to get a letter.

With best love to you both

Harry

Clearly Harry is not pleased with the pay situation. He should be receiving 7 shillings (£0.35) a week with a deduction of 1^1/2d (£0.006) for 'insurance'. (Who says that the military mind has no sense of humour?) By keeping back some of his pay, the Army would have been ensuring that Harry was saving well over a £1 a month – more than £50 at today's values.

The war diary, meanwhile, is still detailing training, as well as a few sporting activities besides some more serious work:

> 6th–12th [March] Bn. relieved the 9th Yorkshire Regt in the line on the MONTELLO (Right Sector, Divl. Front), becoming Support Bn in the Brigade. Musketry, live bombing, grenade throwing, firing the Lewis Gun and training in Bayonet Fighting Course were carried out whilst in those billets.
>
> Specialists were trained under their own officers. A Cross Country run was held on the 10th inst and various football matches were played between companies and platoons. On 10th inst Working Parties were supplied to the Right Front Line Battalion, to improve the Second Line.

Then, in the middle of March, the battalion, having received new orders, left the Piave front, setting off on a lengthy march to the west, to take its place on the Asiago Plateau in the Dolomite Mountains.

During the time on the Piave, the 9th York and Lancasters had been in the front line or in support for a total of around twenty-five days. Four days had been spent marching to Mount Grappa and back. Much of the rest of the time was spent in training, with a significant proportion of that directed towards 'hill fighting'. The battalion had prepared well for its next location.

CHAPTER 9

ASIAGO – SPRING AND SUMMER 1918

SO THE MEN OF THE battalion marched away from the Piave front, heading west, the same direction they had taken a month earlier on the march to Mount Grappa. This time they kept going, moving to a different terrain and climate. After two days' marching across the Venetian Plain, motorized transport took them away from the flat country up into the mountains, on to the Asiago Plateau. The weather in the mountains was extremely cold, wet and snowy, although in a month or so it would certainly change for the better. The war diary entry recording the move shows that the battalion was in good physical condition, and with good morale:

> *15th to 16th* [March] *battalion moved by march route to CASTELFRANCO on 15th inst & proceeded to BOLZANO the following day. The second day's march was long & tedious but no man fell out on either day.*

We can see from Harry's letter below that they marched 25 miles (40km) in two days. One of the 'interior economy' (see Glossary) sessions must have determined that Harry was due for a new pair of boots, hardly ideal for a long march, as military boots take a good deal of breaking in. During the halt at Castelfranco at the end of the first day's march the men must have had some time to visit local shops, as Harry was able to buy a postcard, which he sent to Jack with a letter after the next day's march had ended. Castelfranco is a small town even today, and it must therefore have been quite an event to have several hundred British soldiers arrive for the night. (Then again, perhaps it was a standard stopping-off point for troops on the move, in which case the locals would have sorted out how to maximize profits from the 'visitors'.) Harry's letter two days later is long and, given the likelihood of it being censored, relatively informative.

March 17th/1918
32507/9 Batt York and Lanc Regt., C. Company,
12 Platoon L.G.S., I.E.F

Dear Jack

I was pleased to receive your letter and tin of salmon. It is now Sunday night and it as been very hot we have had church parade this afternoon as we where all busy this morning cleaning up. We have just finished two days march, just over forty kilos so we had a good march and I had a pair of new boots so I went through it but I stuck it. I think we shall stay here a bit now, but we might get to a different part of the line. We had a grand place for scenery when last we were in the line, well the support line we were on Mountbello [Montebello?] *Hills I think that is what they call them. The mountains on one side and we could see right over the venetian plains for miles all fine country it was these plains what the Germans wanted when they made their advance. the Italians releived us when we were in the line they do seem a windy lot as soon as they got in the Austrians started to shell a bit, they all get in dug outs and they would not move. I don't know how they would go on up Ypres. The country is alright but I don't think much to the people a lot of the Italian soldier can speak English as they come from New York or some part of the States. If you see a small book any time which would help me with the Italian Language I should be very pleased if you would send it. I am glad you are both keeping well and I hope they are going on alright at home. I think it will be hot here in summer as some parts of the day now it is awful. We are having a quite time here, well it is a picnic against France. We cant grumble at the rations we are getting out here but of course it is the same thing over and over again. they are sending them on leave from Italy but I dont expect I shall get one for another three or four months yet time for the war to finish by then. I get your papers regular now and I noticed the piece you marked out in the guardian* [newspaper]. *I am sending you a view, I have been to this place a time or two. Write back as soon as possible and let me know how you are getting on.*

With best Love to you both
Harry

Below is the 'view' that Harry sent to Jack. It would appear that a battalion censor has done some work on the name of the place, scoring through the printed words, although it is possible that Harry did it in a half-hearted way in case the censor looked at it.

Harry is not too impressed with the Italian soldiers. Of course, he is by now a battle-hardened veteran, whereas many of the Italian troops were untried, having been hastily drafted in after the catastrophic losses – especially in prisoners – of the Caporetto battle. He will be used to the idea of shelling and, while having respect for the shells, would have arrived at a state of mind that accepted that situation. Italy, he writes, is a picnic against France, but he has no realistic hope of being granted leave any time soon.

Sadly, I have no idea whether he did manage to learn any Italian; nor do I know what was in the article from, I assume, the *Manchester Guardian* (now *The Guardian*) that Jack had sent him.

Quite a good indicator of the relative quietness of this sector of the Italian front is the fact that Harry is able to write more, and fuller, letters, and even the war diary seems almost verbose compared with its entries during the battalion's service at Ypres.

Harry's postcard from Castelfranco, showing the rather feeble attempt at censorship.

17th–24th [March] *Bn in Billets in BOLZANO – the whole Bn was bathed on 17th inst. A Junior N.C.Os class was formed at Bn Hdqrs. instruction being given in Musketry, Lewis Gun, Map Reading and Drill. The class was successful chiefly in increasing the specialised knowledge of the young N.C.Os. The Bn concentrated on Company Drill, Physical Training, Bayonet Fighting and Musketry; each day's programme terminated with 15 minutes ceremonial drill. Specialists were trained by their own officers – the Scouts were instructed in Semaphore Signalling daily. Subaltern officers* [junior officers below the rank of captain] *were similarly instructed by the Signalling officer. A successful Sports meeting was held on the 23rd inst. On 24th inst.* [a Sunday] *the Bn attended a Brigade Church Parade.*

March 21st/1918

32507/9 Batt York and Lanc Regt., C. Company,

12 Platoon L.G.S., I.E.F

Dear Kate

Just a line to let you know that I am going on alright and I am pleased that you are keeping well. I have had a letter from Jack and one from Ethel, they are all going on alright except for the food problem which bothers them a bit. the weather here is grand very hot during the day but very cold at night. Jack is sending Willie a present for is birthday which is saturday. I have sent him and Connie a card or two I hope they like them. I am pleased that you write often as I am always glad of a letter from you. I think I shall get a leave sometime this summer if I have good luck. I will write again soon.

With Love from

Harry

A card that Harry sent to Connie from Italy.

Four days after Harry's latest letter to Kate, the 9th York and Lancasters are on the move again:

25th to 26th Battalion moved by march route to SARCEDO – the following day was devoted to interior economy.
27th Bn. moved by motor lorries to Italian hutments at GRANEZZA.

The use of lorries for the later stage of the journey must have been very welcome. The men had marched across the plain from Montebelluna, but were fortunate to get this motor transport for the significant climb into the mountains.

28th–30th [March] Bn relieved the 28th[?] Italian Regiment in the line, becoming Right Battalion. 'A', 'C' & 'B' Companies were in the front line and 'D' Company in Reserve. The whole of the town was very quiet – little work was done apart from cleaning up and improving sanitary conditions which were very bad. Two patrols were sent out nightly, sometimes three; on two occasions they came in contact with the enemy; much useful information was obtained both by patrols and observation. Major D Lewis D.S.O. M.C. left the Bn on 29th inst to proceed to England to attend a Senior Officers Course at Aldershot.
[Easter Day] 31st Bn was relieved by 11th W Yorks, moving to huts at LANGABISA, and becoming Reserve Bn.
SICKNESS;– During March the average daily attendance at Sick Parade was 25, the prevailing disease being I.C.T. [inflamed connective tissue – probably trench foot].

The end of March and the start of April sees the battalion in training again:

1st–4th [April] Bn in reserve in hutments at LANGABISA. During this period training in HILL FIGHTING was carried out in its various phases.

Two days later, Harry wrote to both Kate and Jack:

April 2/4/1918

32507/ 9 York & Lancs., C Company,

12 Platoon L.G.S., I.E.F.

Dear Kate

I have just got your letter dated 24/ I also got the money alright. Postal orders are alright. I have also had a letter from Jack and one from Ethel. Ethel told me that Jack had sent Willie a shilling [£0.05] for his birthday, it will soon be Connie's now. The weather here is very cold we have had frost and snow and it has been raining now two days, but still we are alright, it is very quiet not like beening in France. I am always glad to get a letter from you I have not been able to write any letters lately, but if you don't get one you will know the reason so you can write a line every week. I am pleased they are all keeping in good health at home and that dad does not get any worse. I will try and write you a long letter next time I write. Could you send me a stick of shaving shop and a piece of washing soap next time you write.

With Best Love

Harry

April 2/4/1918

32507/ 9 York & Lancs., C Company,

12 Platoon L.G.S., I.E.F.

Dear Jack

Just a line to let you know I am going on alright. I was pleased to get your letter and to hear that you both are keeping well. We have had some frost and snow out here, but it as been raining for two days. I have had a letter from home and they told me you had sent Willie a birthday present. Things are very quiet out here a bit different to being out in France. things seems to be a bit rough out there now, but I hope things will change. I will write again in a few days and let you know a bit more news.

With Best Love to you both

Harry

P.S. Could you send a few envelopes and writing paper

The front on the Asiago Plateau was not inactive, however, as war diary entries for the following weeks show:

8th to 11th [April] *Battalion in the Line. Our patrols were very active nightly and on the night of 9–10 a fighting patrol consisting of 2 Officers and 20 O.R. succeeded in capturing 2 prisoners – just outside the enemy's wire at MORAR. The patrol returned safely with the two prisoners without loss. 2/Lt F Flory was slightly wounded in the foot.*

14th Battn at MARE. 2/Lts F FLORY and W MEAD were awarded the MILITARY CROSS for conspicuous gallantry on the night of the 9th, 10th of April.

On the same date 17558 Pte J Shillington received the DCM [Distinguished Conduct Medal]

10983 a/s [Acting Sergeant] *V.G. Stokes received Bar to MM* [i.e. a second MM]

15819 Pte R. Morgan received the MM

235382 Pte W Knight received the MM

16th to 19th at GRENAZZA. In spite of very inclement weather, training was carried on continuously.

19th Battn moved to FARA area using the mountain mule tracks. Battn in billets by 3 p.m. having moved off at 8.45 a.m.

20th Battn moved off at 9.30 a.m marching to camp at VILLA VERLA. Battn in camp at 1 p.m.

21st Battn moved off at 9.45 a.m. and marched to billets at GRUMO taking the route over the mountains from ISOLA VICENTINA – Very heavy rainstorm during the whole of the march but the Commanding Officer arranged for fires to be lighted in all billets on arrival & special drying rooms were allocated in addition so that all men and their clothes were thoroughly dried and no ill effects were experienced. Arrived in billets at 5.30 p.m.

This would not have been an easy trek. The battalion set out in the mountains, its destination on the plains below Mount Grappa. The weather would have made the march very challenging, although the fires and 'drying rooms' at journey's end would have been welcome. The 'mountains' on the route from Isola Vicente to Grumo are modest in comparison to the terrain the men had left. In his next letter, Harry describes some of the discomforts the battalion had undergone. He had also had news, which I think he had expected for some time, about his father.

April 22nd 1918
32507/9th Batt Y & L Regt., C. Company,
12 Platoon L.G.S.

Dear Jack

I am sorry I have not been able to write to you lately but we have been on a fresh front on the Asiago Plateau it was different altogether from the Piave. We went up the mountain first time in motor cars [lorries] as far as we could get. When we was on the plains it was very hot but when we got to the trenches it was knee deep in snow and freezing. After we had been up a bit it started to rain, we got wet through time after time. There was nothing doing only patrols we had a rough time now and again, we had to do outpost duty, we should be about two hundred yards in front of our own wire, you can bet what it was like out there in the rain and snow but we are down on the plains now and I am in the best of health. By the time you get this letter I shall have been out here [i.e. on active service abroad, not out in Italy] *12 months altogether. I was rather upset to hear that father is dead. I had a letter from Ilkeston* [presumably from Ethel] *telling me that he had died April 7th. I have not been able to send any letters for about three weeks so they will wonder where I have got too. I am pleased you keep writing to me, I hope you are both keeping in the best of health. We don't seem to be getting on very well with the war in France* [by now, the Ludendorff Offensive, which had been launched on 21 March, had made huge inroads against the British and French armies in Belgium and France] *it would not surprise me if some of our chaps dont have to go back. Write back as soon as you can and let me know all the news you can. I suppose you have had the Zepps* [bombing raids by German airships, generally known as 'Zeppelins'] *around your way again. I hope they are all keeping well* at Ilkeston. I have met one or two fellows from Ilkeston and one from Kimberly [Kimberley, Nottinghamshire, not far from Ilkeston] in our battalion. I will write again soon I don't think we shall go up the mountains when we go in the trenches again, it does seem strange to be up above the clouds, I can tell you we see some fine sights, you would like to be here in peace time for a holiday. I am going to write to Kate now.

With best Love to you both.

Harry

The letter to Jack of 22 April 1918.

The battalion war diary does make some occasional mention of the rain and snow, but on the whole the troops took such things in their stride. A 'rough time' is Harry's gentle way of saying that there has been some significant military action.

The paper Harry used this time is rather different. On the front is printed 'FOR SCRIBBLING OR NOTES ONLY', on the reverse, 'Question . . . . . . Write only on this side of the paper, and not on either margin.' Presumably, Jack, the former schoolmaster, had sent him some old examination answer sheets.

At about this time, one of the four other divisions that had travelled with 23rd Division from Flanders in the autumn returned there to strengthen the Allied defence against the devastating German offensive that had already won significant gains. Harry may have heard about that and been a little concerned that the 23rd might be ordered to follow – not a welcome prospect.

April 26th/4/1918
32507/9th Batt York & Lancs Regt., C Company,
12 Platoon L.G.S., I.E.F.

Dear Kate

Just a line to let you know that I am going on alright and that I am in good health. I had a letter from Ilkeston telling me about dad, I was very sorry to hear it but it as been wonderful how he as kept up. The weather here as been very changeable just lately plenty of rain but we have had it hot now and again. We can get plenty to eat were we are just now, such as fruit and eggs. The scenery is also very pretty. did you get over to Ilkeston, if you did, how long did you stop. I have had a letter from Jack and he told me that Mr Thomas's eldest son had been killed in Palestine that is the second son he has lost it is very hard lines and I was sorry to hear it. They were both officers. one was in the West Riding's Batt [a Territorial battalion of the Duke of Wellington's (West Riding) Regiment]. *There is only one son left but he is only about 17^1/2 years* [in most cases, the minimum age for the armed services was eighteen].

I have put a letter for you in Ethels envelope I hope you get it alright, let me know if you get it. Write every week if you can, it does not matter if it is only just a line or two.

With Best Love
Harry

April 30th 1918
32507/ 9th Batt Y & L., C. Company,
12 Platoon L.G.S., I.E.F.

Dear Jack

I am writing a few lines to you hoping that you are both in good health. It is a long time since I wrote to you till this week so I expect you will get two letters at about the same time [in fact, his last letter to Jack had been sent eight days earlier]. *I should be pleased if you will send me a small book on the Lewis Gun and one which I think is called the soldier it gives you all information about guards, salutes and all army regulations etc. if you cant get one, send the best you can. I expect we shall have to do guards out here. I think they are getting on a bit better at Ilkeston now* [after Harry's father's death]. *I don't know when I shall get a leave, all leave is stopped out here for a bit. I hope you got that letter telling you I was amongst the snow and rain on the Asiago Plateau front, it did seem strange to be amongst the mountains for a month. I was very sorry to hear that Mr Thomas's son as got killed it is very sad. Write as often as you can as I cant get letters off very well when I am in the line.*

With Best Love to you both
Harry

It seems a little strange, if commendable, that Harry should be asking for books about military procedure. I can understand his interest in a booklet about the Lewis gun, but I am quite certain that, like most infantrymen, he wasn't a fan of saluting and drills.

The war diary entry for the end of April closes the month with a wonderfully down-to-earth entry:

30th Sickness, Admissions to hospital were the LOWEST on record for the past SIX months. Sick parades have been above the average. The prevailing diseases being IMPETIGO and BOILS.

At the end of April 1918 the battalion moved to new barracks at Arzignano, at the foot of the mountains about ten miles (16km) west of Vicenza, where it carried out intensive training.

1–12 [May] *Battalion in billets at ARZIGNANO from 1st to the 12th. During this period training in hill fighting was carried on assiduously. A large field opposite the H.Q. mess of the 9th York & Lancaster Regt. was leased. Col D S Rumbolt* [Rumbold] *of the 9th and Col Watford of the 8th York & Lancaster Regt defraying the expense. The companies were able to drill and exercise, and during their stay, a highly successful inter Battalion Sports Meeting was held. All the men were bathed and supplied with complete 'changes'* [of uniform and clothing] *at the Brigade Baths on two occasions. rifle ranges were constructed and all men practised in MUSKETRY. A special programme of work for scouts was drawn up including five nights for weak* [sic] *night operations. A Recreation Room was established, games, concerts provided.*

Still on the plains, the battalion was evidently short of space for training and so, amazingly, the CO and his opposite number from the 8th Battalion paid for the rent of a field. I find this strange. I had assumed that the Army would, with British good manners, have simply apologized to the local inhabitants for the inconvenience, and taken what was needed to fight the war.

May 8th 1918

32507/ 9th Batt Y & Lancs Reg., C Company,

12 Platoon L.G.S., I.E.F.

Dear Jack

I have just received two letters and small packett I was very pleased with them. I hope you got my letters asking for a book or two, if so will you send them on as soon as possible. I have had a letter from Ilkeston they are all getting on as well as can be expected, which I was very pleased to hear. I think Connie and Willie will miss grandad but they will soon forget. We have had a lot of rain here lately, but when the sun does shine it is very hot, things in the gardens and fields are looking very well, you can see small bunches of grapes forming on some of the vines already and I have seen one or two lemons on the trees, it must be fine to have a summer out here and see all the fruit ripen. I was very pleased that Mr Leverton was at dad's funeral it was very good of him. I think I will write a few lines to him.

> *With best love to you both*
> *Harry*

Near the end of the first fortnight of May, the battalion made its way on foot back up the mountains to the Asiago Plateau, where once again it took its turn in the line.

> *12th to 25th* [May] *Battalion in the line. New positions selected and constructed. Patrols – offensive and defensive – were sent out nightly; also reconnaissance patrols. and much valuable information was gained with regard to the enemy's work and disposition. In spite of this continuous activity, the Battalion was fortunate enough to have NO casualties of any kind. About the middle of the month, a fever which had already attacked the 8th Battn, broke out and spread rapidly from Bn H.Q. to 'B' and 'C' Coys. then to 'A' Coy and finally to 'D' Coy. At no time dangerous, the illness was marked by sudden very high temperatures lasting from two to four days followed by a period of lassitude from six to ten days. Isolative camps were established and every hut and bivouac thoroughly disinfected and fumigated. By the end of the month the sick list was becoming normal. On the 15th of the month, the well which had been supplying washing and cooking water was reported to have run dry but the Commanding Officer immediately instituted extra sections of water-carrying mules and practically no inconvenience was felt.*

The war diary is clearly referring to an outbreak of influenza, for the 'Spanish Flu' epidemic was to be a horrible feature of the summer, and on through that year and the next. The strain that was afflicting Harry's battalion sounds quite mild – most unpleasant, however, in a trench environment. In the end, the pandemic was to kill some twenty million people worldwide between 1918 and 1920. It was probably because the men of the battalion were by now extremely fit, and were not serving in the much harsher conditions of the Western Front, that they escaped relatively lightly, for flu was to kill tens of thousands of soldiers in all the combatant armies in the dying months of the war. Harry's next letter, however, makes no mention of it.

May 21th [sic] 1918
32507/ 9th Batt York & Lancs., C Company,
12 Platoon L.G.S., I.E.F.

Dear Jack
I have received your letter and books alright. The small book is very handy as it does not take up much room. I thank you very much for sending them. I have just had a letter from Kate and she is getting on alright. We are still in the same place only it is a bit warmer this time up, and not so quiet, but I am going on alright. You will see that we have a Y.M. up here but it is only a very small one. If you dont get a letter from me every week, keep writing as it is very hard at times to get letters away. I did not see any processions at Easter as we were in an out of the way place but there would be plenty no doubt. They go to church at all times here. I have seen them going at five in the morning and bells ringing at three. Every body here seems to go to church regular. we see some strange sights out here, but the scenery is very pretty. I guess Willie would fancy himself when writing to you. I will write again as soon as possible. I am please that you are both getting on alright and keeping well.
With best love
Harry

Harry's reference to 'a Y.M.' means, of course, the YMCA, which during that war provided canteen and other facilities – including writing paper – for troops at the front. I have been unable to discover whether the book Harry received from Jack was about the Lewis gun, or about military procedure. It is clear from his letter, too, that, unlike in Flanders, civilian life in Italy, even close to the front line, seems to go on around the troops.

The first days of June were spent in quite intensive training before the battalion moved into the line once more.

> *11th* [June] *The Battalion relieved the 8th battalion, K.O.Y.L.I. in the left sector, Right Brigade front: relief was complete at 8 am. Very heavy rainfall during the day and night. By night, the outpost line was held by patrols* [positions in advance of the front line, manned in order to provide warning of enemy activity, especially an attack].
>
> *12th The front line trenches and support positions were improved.*

Already under strength, the battalion was also weakened by the influenza attacks. The enemy, however, with extra divisions available from the Eastern Front following Russia's withdrawal from the war in March 1918, recognized that a decisive offensive in Italy had every chance of proving successful. The plan was to attack on both the Asiago Plateau and the Piave front at the same time. Harry's battalion found itself in the line at Asiago as the activity increased, duly recorded by the war diary:

> *13th Considerable improvement in weather conditions. At night, our defensive patrol was engaged by hostile rifle fire, bombs and mortars from the vicinity of S. AVE, one casualty being sustained.*
>
> *14th Increase in reciprocal artillery fire [i.e. shelling by both sides] throughout the day. By night the outpost line was held by patrols.*

A really helpful sketch map is included in the war diary of the 11th Sherwood Foresters (Nottinghamshire and Derbyshire Regiment), another of the battalions in 70 Brigade, giving an excellent view of dispositions as the Austro-Hungarians attacked on the morning of 15 June (see page 144). The 9th York and Lancasters hold the positions to the left. According to the battalion's own war diary, some effort had been made to improve the defensive positions.

As the artillery activity increased, the defenders would be aware that an attack was certainly imminent. The action started before dawn on the 15th with a bombardment, including gas shells. The battalion's forward patrol, as reported in the war diary

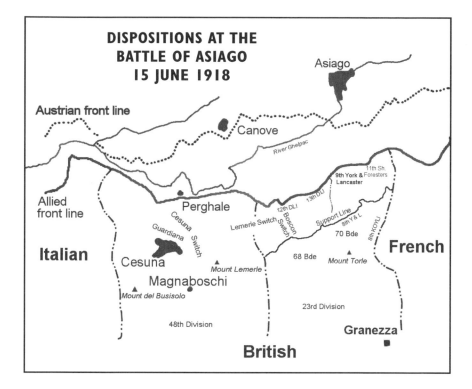

DISPOSITIONS AT THE BATTLE OF ASIAGO 15 JUNE 1918

Asiago

Austrian front line

Canove

River Ghelpac

11th Sh.
9th York & Foresters
Lancaster

Allied front line

Perghale

Cesuna
Guardiana Switch
Cesuna Switch

Lemerle Switch
12th DLI
Boscon Switch
13th DLI
Support Line
8th Y & L
8th KOYLI

70 Bde

Italian

Cesuna

Mount Lemerle

68 Bde
Mount Torle

French

Magnaboschi

Mount del Busisolo

23rd Division

48th Division

Granezza

British

entry below, seems to have been overrun by the advancing Austro-Hungarian troops as the attack developed.

> *15th 3am Enemy opened bombardment on our front system, lachrymatory [tear] gas being used. Our patrol of one officer and twenty other ranks was surprised by the enemy, only two men escaping to our lines.*
>
> *5.30am to 7.30 am Enemy advanced to the attack, but only succeeded in getting within 100 yards of our wire, where he was disorganised and checked, enemy bombardment was continued.*
>
> *8.30am Enemy in artillery formation* [i.e. advancing in small groups rather than extended line to minimize casulties from shellfire] *advanced between S.W.of ASIAGO and EDELWEISS SPUR forming up in line on reverse slope* [the side of a hill away from the enemy] *of GUARDINALTI ridge. M.G's* [machine

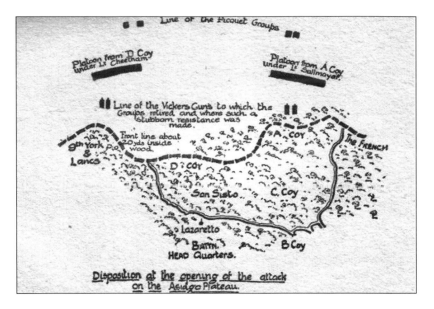

The sketch map of the action on the Asiago Plateau, 15 June 1918, from the war diary of the 11th Battalion, the Sherwood Foresters, and showing Harry's battalion on the left flank.

guns] *were pushed well forward and opened rapid fire at intervals. 10.30am Situation became normal. Reciprocal artillery fire was maintained. Enemy casualties were apparently heavy, stretcher bearers carrying back their wounded during the day.*

The morning dawned damp and foggy, and the tear gas would have added to the defenders' problems. The attack was, with some difficulty, beaten off; the near total loss of the battalion's forward patrol would have been a blow (as they were 'surprised' by the enemy, with luck most of them were captured). The war diary states that machine guns were pushed well forward. The sketch map (opposite) indicates that these were probably Vickers machine guns rather than the lighter battalion Lewis guns. The diary entry is somewhat ambiguous, however, as there are other references to the Austro-Hungarian forces pushing machine guns forward of the main assault.

While the Austro-Hungarian Army succeeded in breaking through the front line in several places, the 9th Battalion beat them off in their sector of the line. On their right, the 11th Sherwood Foresters temporarily lost the forward line of trenches but counter-attacked and recovered them during the day. The defensive tactics at this stage of the war had evolved to produce successive lines of (relatively) lightly defended trenches rather than a single substantial front-line trench. If the first line of trenches was successfully attacked, then the second became the new front line, and so on.

It was still light in the early evening when the enemy attacked again. The war diary records what happened in understated terms:

> *6pm Enemy, numbering more than one thousand, advanced in artillery formation between RODIGHIERI and OBA, forming up under cover between ASIAGO and SILVEGNAR.*
> *9pm Approximately 200 enemy retired in scattered parties from GUARDINALTI ridge.*
> *10pm Up to this hour, forty of the enemy were brought in to our lines. Desultory artillery fire throughout the night.*

For the battalion, it had been a nerve-racking, but successful, evening with some enemy prisoners to show for it. The attack was important to the Austro-Hungarian forces, making it almost inevitable that the first day's lack of success should be followed by a second attempt to break through on 16 May. The day began quietly enough, however:

> *16th 6am Two hostile light field guns were brought in to our lines from the vicinity of GUARDINALTI. Later four machine guns, three flammenwerfer, one case of gas shells, ammunition etc, were brought in by our small reconnoitring parties. Situation quiet throughout the day.*

This time the main attack came in the evening.

> *9.45pm Enemy S.O.S.* [signal flare, in this case indicating the start of the assault] *followed by artillery barrage on our lines. At*

the same time, hostile M.G.'s in advanced positions opened fire on our lines.

10pm Small parties of the enemy getting within 100 yards of our wire in centre of Battalion front fired rifle grenades and Very lights in large numbers, into our trenches. Cheering was heard from 'no man's land'. [A rifle grenade was equipped with a metal rod to fit inside a rifle barrel; fired using a blank cartridge, they travelled further than hand-thrown grenades. Very lights were signal flares fired from a flare pistol, which burned with intense heat and light and were difficult to extinguish.]

10.15pm Battalion on our left fired S.O.S. [to call for artillery support] *artillery barrage opening on line POSLEN – GUARDINALTI – VLA DAL BRUN.*

11.30pm Situation became quieter; hostile Very lights in large numbers, showed enemy parties retiring between MORAR and AVE.

It must have been something of a relief to the defenders as it became clear that the attack had failed. The large numbers of flares put up were probably to provide illumination for enemy troops trying to find their way back to their lines from no man's land.

17th Prisoners, wounded and otherwise, were brought in during the day, making a total of three officers and ninety-one other ranks. Relieved by the 10th Battalion Duke of Wellington Regiment. Relief was completed by 5pm. Battalion marched to hutments in GRANEZZA.

A couple of days later, safely out of the front line, Harry sends Jack quite a striking account of the attack.

June 19/1918
32507/ 9th Batt., York & Lancs Regt.,
C Coy 12 platoon, L.G.S., I.E.F.

    Dear Jack

I hope you are getting on alright. I have received the book and was very pleased with it. I have not received a letter for a long time. things have been a bit rough out here just lately something unusual after beening so quiet. Our Coy was in close support about 200 yards behind front line we were not wanted in the front line so we did not have to fire. I can tell you support line is worst than the front. The fight started about 3 oclock in the morning and Johnny Austrian started to come over about 7 o clock. Well he did get a reception I can tell you, them in the front line simply mowed them down and he got no farther than the wire. I went in the front line during the day to have a look when things had quietened down. The prisoners are the poorest lot I have seen and told us they thought that they were going to meet the Italians and where surprised to see our lads in the trenches. it was a big attack and he meant breaking through if he could. The prisoners had plenty of money, all notes and was pleased to be made prisoners, well the biggest part of them. They were a mixed lot Austrians, Hungarians and a large number of Rumanians. there objective was to get on to the plain but I can tell you he got a good beating especially on our divisional front. I shall be glad to see you all again and I hope you are both keeping in good health. I shall be able to tell you more when I see you. I hope this year sees the finish of the war, but I think that the enemy is more fed up than what we are. I have had a letter from home and pleased to say they are keeping well. Write as often as you can.

With Love to you both

Harry

(P.S.) I am putting an Austrian note in I hope you get it.

The successful defence of the Asiago Plateau must have been a great boost to the defenders' morale. A couple of sentences in Harry's letter show how positive he must have felt: 'The prisoners are the poorest lot I have seen and told us they thought that they were going to meet the Italians and where [*sic*] surprised to see our lads in the trenches.' 'I think that the enemy is more fed up than what we are,' he adds, reflecting on a possible end to the war. (The Austro-Hungarian banknote, sent in a separate envelope with the letter, survived in excellent condition.)

The Austro-Hungarian banknote that Harry sent home.

Astonishingly, he went into the front line after the action 'to have a look'. By now, of course, he was a veteran infantryman, confident of his battalion's ability to beat off any attacks. In Flanders, a non-essential visit to the front-line trench simply wouldn't have been considered. It was not a place for sightseeing.

Between the war diary and Harry's letter we get a good picture of the two days' fighting. The offensive was a disaster for the Austro-Hungarian forces, which suffered heavy casualties and made no progress. Even at the start of the battles the attacking troops were ill-equipped and in poor condition after a winter in the mountains (as is confirmed by Harry's account).

On the plains, along the Piave front, the enemy met with a similar lack of success. There was, initially, some progress at the eastern, seaward, end of the river and to the north, but the rain in the mountains earlier in the month made the river a formidable obstacle for men and supplies and an effective block to any retreat. Consequently, the Austro–Hungarian losses were severe. In addition, the attackers found that the Italian Army was no longer the demoralized and poorly led force of nine months earlier. To compound their problems, the defensive lines were stiffened with tough, experienced British and French divisions, drawn from the Western Front. By the middle of June, after failure on both Italian fronts, it was quite clear that the Austro-Hungarian Army was disintegrating.

The battalion's part in throwing back the enemy offensive on the Asiago Plateau was recognized later in the month, as the war diary records:

Routine orders dated 25-6-1918 and 28-6-1918 contained the following awards for gallantry and distinguished conduct in the field during the operations of the 15-6-1918:-

MILITARY CROSS
Captain J.P. Shaw R.A.M.C. [Royal Army Medical Corps] attached York & Lancaster Regiment
Captain L. Lester; 2/Lieut. A. Hirst; 2/Lieut. J Ferguson

DISTINGUISHED CONDUCT MEDAL
12/1246 C.S.M. J.A. Willoughby
241359 L/Cpl. E. Naylor M.M.

BAR TO MILITARY MEDAL
240660 L/Cpl E. Brock M.M.

MILITARY MEDAL
17068 L/Cpl West J.; 34879 L/Cpl Stead H.
34582 Pte Dalenay; 235466 Pte. (A/Cpl) Boon J.R.

Sickness During the month of June, admissions to hospital were normal, the general health of the Battalion being good. Prevailing diseases were IMPETAGO [sic] and BOILS.

The beginning of July found the battalion out of the line, and Harry was able to write home again, this time to Kate as well as Jack.

July 2th [sic]/1918
32507/ 9th Batt Y & L.,
C Coy 12 Platoon, L.G.S., I.E.F.

Dear Kate

I have received your letter and the papers with the writing pad. I was very pleased with it. I have had a letter from Ethel and she says they are getting on alright at home. The weather here is very unsettled and we get plenty of rain. You were right when you say we have been busy out here just lately but I am pleased to say I am going on alright and in good health and I hope to keep so. I am pleased to here that Jack is getting on alright I had a letter from him last week. I hope Annie does not leave home and go to work, well I think she would be better at home. I think she might be able to find a bit of work to suit her in time. Write as often as you can and let me know how they are all getting on.

With best Love

Harry

July 2th/1918
32507/ 9th Batt Y & L.
C Coy 12 Platoon, L.G.S., I.E.F.

Dear Jack

Just a line to let you know that I am alright and in good health. The weather here is very unsettled and we got plenty of rain. I hope you received my last letter in the green envelope [i.e. one that avoided the battalion censor]. *Let me know if you have. I am pleased to hear they are going on alright at home and keeping in good health. I think Annie is worrying herself about getting work but I don't think she as any need to both* [bother?]. *You will be glad to hear that Willie is getting a fine lad. I had a letter from Mr Leverton telling me about him. I will write a soon and let you know a bit more news. Hoping that you are both keeping in good health.*

With Best Love to you both

Harry

(P.S.) Send a paper or two

This letter gives another clue that Harry is quite optimistic about the war's progress. He is asking for newspapers, almost certainly expecting to get more good news about the possibility of the war ending. By now, on the Western Front, the tide had turned in the Allies' favour, and the Germans in turn were beginning to be pressed hard as Ludendorff's offensive, itself a last-ditch strategy to win the war before American forces and resources could take full effect, began to peter out.

The war diary of the 9th York and Lancasters has nothing to say about a possible end to the war, but records that there was still a fair bit of activity on the Asiago front.

> *5th to 11th* [July] – *Battalion in the line. By day, work on the defensive system was continued, and by night our outpost positions were improved, a considerable amount of wire being erected in front thereof. Patrols were sent out by night. Hostile shelling was intermittent during our tour in the line.*

I have placed Harry's next letter from Italy after the war diary entry for 5–11 July, as I am sure it is misdated.

> *July 8th 1918 [16 July?]*
> *32507/9th Batt Y & L., C Coy 12 Platoon*
> *L G S., I.E.F.*

> Dear Kate

> *I was glad to receive your letter dated 7th. Sorry I not wrote this last week but you see we have been up the mountains for about 7 or 8 weeks and all the envelopes were stuck. I hope we get down now for two or three weeks. We have had some trying times up in the front line on what we call sacrifice post up in front of our own wire but I am glad to say we got off alright we only went out after dark till morning. Glad to hear they are going on alright at home, I think it would be best for Annie to stay at home and wait for a bit of work. I have had a letter from Mr Leverton. I bet Willie fancies himself with his new clothes. We have got some very thin khaki and those big helmets* [sun helmets, also known as pith helmets or solar topis, and usually issued for tropical service] *they are alright out here as it is very hot on the plains. I might get home on leave late in September if I have*

good luck but I hope the war will soon finish. I think it as been on long enough. I am glad that you are keeping well as I am in the pink at present. The scenery out here is grand it would be alright in peace time for a holiday. we are half way up the mountain now and can see for miles along the plains it does look well. The people out here have some funny ways and not so clean as English, but in towns they are alright they are all Roman Catholics out here. Write as often as you can and let me know how you are getting on send a book or two if you can.

With best Love
Harry

Everything points to Harry dating this letter wrongly. The war diary tells us the summer kit wasn't issued until 14 July and that the battalion was in the front line on the 8th – letter writing would not have been easy. I would guess that it was written at about the same time as Harry's 16 July letter to Jack, not least because its content is very similar. It also tells us that letters were taking about a week from being written in England to being delivered in Italy – not too bad for a wartime postal service, under which the General Post Office had to transfer letters for soldiers to the Army's postal service, for onward transmission to any one of thousands of serving units.

Still close to the mountains, but away from the front line on the edge of the plains, the weather is obviously warm enough to justify the issue of tropical kit and the 'big helmets'. It seems likely that there were plans to move the 9th York and Lancasters back to the plains; certainly Harry thinks that is a possibility. This is the war diary's record of the issue of tropical clothing to the men:

14th Church services were held in the morning. Khaki-drill clothing was issued. The Commanding Officer, accompanied by O.C. Companies, reconnoitred the 7th Divisional front.

There was a small problem with the khaki-drill clothing, which was lighter in colour than the standard-issue uniform. While it was fine in a desert environment, at night it showed much paler than the background and the soldiers were easily seen. Harry mentions the thinness of the material in his letter to Jack:

July 16th /18
32507/ 9th Bn Y & L., C Coy 12 platoon,
L.G.S., I.E.F.

Dear Jack

I have received your letters dated 8th July. I was very pleased to get one. We have been up the mountains for about 7 or 8 weeks and I could not get any envelopes they were all stuck so I have not been able to write many letters. We have started to come down so I hope we shall be down for two or three weeks rest. It is very hot on the plains. We have been rigged out with drill khaki it is very thin alright for summer, we have also got those big helmets. I am glad to hear that you are all getting on well.

Some of or chaps were very bad last month with a complaint we called mountain fever. I had a slight attack but I did not go sick [i.e. report in sick]. *all the use goes out of your legs, sore throat and cough but you soon get well, we were isolated for a fortnight but we are alright now. I should not be surprised if we don't get on another front again, perhaps the Piave. I am in good health at present. We have had some trying jobs lately in front line on advance posts what they call sacrifice posts out all night about a thousand yards in front of our own wire and we have to stick it and only retire in case of a big bombardment, any minor raids we have to stick at all costs. This last month it has been something like France only the Austrians front line is at least two kilos away. I have had a letter from Ilkeston and they are getting on well they are making Willie a suit or two so I expect he will fancy himself. I have also had a letter from Mr Leverton. Hope you will keep writing every week as I am always glad to get a letter.*

With best Love to you both
Harry

We can see that the tactical situation is quite different from that in Flanders, where the enemy lines were less than 200 yards ahead – and sometimes less than 100 yards. The advance listening posts – 'sacrifice posts' – were not at all popular in Flanders either, where they were even more dangerous because of the proximity of the Germans.

August, marking the start of the fifth year of the war, finds Harry still in a cheerfully relaxed frame of mind, as this letter to Jack shows (he may not be quite clear about the detail of *Romeo and Juliet*...):

Aug 4th

32507/ 9th Batt Y & Lancs, C Coy 12 Platoon,

L.G.S., I.E.F.

Dear Jack

I hope you are getting on alright as I am in good health at present. The weather out here is very hot at present and the grapes and the figs are looking well but they are not ripe yet. I expect we shall be up the mountain when they are ready for picking. last time we were up we were there for eight or nine weeks it is a long time to be up and see nothing only plenty of fir trees so I think we have earned four or five weeks rest which I hope we shall get well we have had just over a fortnight now. The scenery is alright here we are at a place were Shakespeare wrote his poem about Romeo and Juliet. There is two castles just above our billets on a big hill and it is said that it was in one of these that he wrote this peace. it would just suit you to have a roam about here, but it is very quiet. I see from the papers that the Americans have arrived in Italy and have been to Rome. I wish they would take us to a place like that were we could see things. I have had a letter from Kate and she said that she was thinking of going home for August and she was going to send Connie to a school at Liverpool. I hope she [Connie] gets on alright it will be hard for her to leave home but I hope she gets treated alright if not she would be better at home. Well it is Sunday today, and the fourth anniversary of the war, we have just been to church service. I think it looks like going on another year although some people think it will be over this year. I hope so at any rate. I expect I shall be getting a leave late on in September or early October, well I hope so. What do you think about the war. Do you think it will be long. We are up at 3.30 A.M. and finish at 9 A.m. Then we have an hour at night, that is while the weather is so hot, and while we are out for a rest. I am sending you a photo or two if you get them will you send one or two to Kate and Annie when you write they are photos [postcards] *of the castle. I have been up to them.*

    With best Love to you both
    Harry

The war diary prosaically records that Harry's hopes of four or five weeks away from the line were vain; nor did the issue of tropical kit last long:

14th [August] *Khaki-drill clothing was withdrawn and service dress clothing issued. The Battalion marched from BERGANA to CAMISINO.*

16th The Battalion relieved the 1st Battalion, South Staffordshire Regt. in the CESUNA SWITCH (left Brigade, left Divisional sector): relief was complete at midnight. Battalion HQrs and 'A' Company were in the CESUNA TUNNEL, the remaining three Companies occupying the SWITCH.

17th & 18th Reciprocal artillery fire during the day. At night a working party from 'A' Company improved PERGHELE TRENCH, and repaired camouflage on CESUNA ROAD.

18th C. of E. Service was held at 3 pm in the CESUNA TUNNEL.

About a month after issue, the hot-weather gear is handed back. The plans must be to send the 9th York and Lancasters and the rest of 23rd Division back into the mountains. Sure enough, Harry's next letter confirms that they have moved back – Cesuna is on the Asiago Plateau, a few miles west of the positions they had held for the battle of 15–16 June. The letter is written on YMCA notepaper, which accounts for the different address layout.

      Reply to: Company C Bat 9th Regt. York & Lancs
                         Aug 19th 1918
                         12 Platoon L. G. S.

    Dear Jack
I hope you got the post cards I sent in my last letter. Ethel is having Willies photo taken so I expect I shall be getting one. We are up the

mountains again now it is much cooler than being on the plains, the worst part about it is getting here it is such a big climb I can tell you, and it takes us a long time to get up we are all beat when we get to the top. The village we are at now used to be occupied by Italians who were well off. they used to come up here in the summer, it was too hot on the plains for them but of course no one lives here now as it has been knocked about a bit. I think the Americans are coming up here, well I hope we are not up this quarter for the winter as it is terribly cold for six or seven months and plenty of snow. I shall be glad to see you all again, but I expect I shall be home on leave sometime in the next month if I have good luck, so I expect to see you. I am glad that you are both keeping in good health as I am pretty well at present. I am sending this letter in Ethel's so I hope you get it alright. Write as often as you can. I am always pleased to get a line from you.

  With best love to you both
  Harry

Harry was a little optimistic about American involvement on the plateau. A small contingent, an infantry regiment, had arrived in the mountains but by this time had been transferred to the Piave front.

While the Austro-Hungarian Army may have been becoming demoralized, it still had plenty of artillery. The war diary notes an increase in activity on the Asiago front:

19th [August] *Little artillery fire during the day: At night the Brigadier General and Brigade Major accompanied the Commanding Officer round the post line in CESUNA SWITCH.*
20th Hostile artillery very active during the day, a number of shells falling in the vicinity of CESUNA. Work on PERGHELE TRENCH was continued.
21st Hostile artillery fire again active, in consequence of which two companies of the 8th Battalion K.O.L.I. [KOYLI] moved down to CESUNA TUNNEL from MAGNABOSCHI.
22nd Artillery quiet during the day. Working parties were continued at night.

Three of the five postcards that Harry sent to Jack early in August 1918.

23rd Considerable increase in enemy artillery fire during the day, a large number of shells falling on the N.W. slope Mt LEMERLE.

We should note Harry's birthday. On 28 August 1918, he was thirty-one years old, and had been on active service for a year and three months, during which time he had not seen his family once. His son, Willie, who was now two and a half years old, he had known for just nine months. There follows a gap in the letters, however. This is certainly due to Harry being granted leave back to England, all the evidence suggesting that he would have had two weeks towards the end of September 1918 back at home.

In general, ordinary soldiers could expect to get around two weeks' home leave each year. Harry has definitely not had leave since he arrived in Italy in late 1917. I initially suspected, but had no firm evidence, that he had been granted leave in August 1917, while serving in Flanders. I have since discovered, however, that there was no leave from that sector at that time. I am amazed that he hasn't made some sort of comment in his letters, given that he had gone without leave for around twenty months.

August turned to September. On the Asiago Plateau, even as Harry was on leave, his unit continued to play its part in the front line.

19th [September] *The Battalion relieved the 8th Battalion York & Lancaster Regiment in the left front sub-sector, right Brigade left Divisional front. 'A', 'B' & 'C' Companies relieved during the morning and 'D' Company (Outpost) at night.*
20th–24th Reciprocal artillery fire day & night. The trench system was improved and a considerable amount of wire erected on forward slope of STAFFORD HILL.

During this period, Harry was away from the war, on leave back in England. While he was away, his battalion shifted from the mountains back down to the plains, where he was to rejoin them.

I would guess that this photograph is the one that Harry mentions in his letter to Jack of 19 August 1918 (I have several copies of it in a box of 'bits & bobs'). Willie certainly looks the right age. I have also received a number of comments from followers of the blog suggesting that Connie is using the chair for support, since it is very likely that the cerebral palsy affected her walking – probably her balance. My sister Anita still has the chair, so the picture may have been taken by a visiting photographer rather than, as was often the case in those days, in a studio. The photograph would have been an expensive item for Ethel and so I think it likely that Kate would have helped out with the cost.

CHAPTER 10

THE ENDGAME

THE ALLIED STAFF, RECOGNIZING that the Austro-Hungarian Army was close to collapse, planned to complete the job with a major offensive on the Piave front. At the end of September, as part of this plan, Harry's battalion was shifted eastwards from the Asiago Plateau to the plains.

The offensive actually began with an attack back on the Asiago Plateau. This was merely a feint which succeeded in drawing the Austro-Hungarians' meagre reserves from the Piave front into the mountains.

On 24 October, the first anniversary of the start of the Battle of Caporetto, the main attack started, in foggy conditions, with the capture of Grave di Papadopoli, a large island in the Piave, about ten miles (16km) north-north-east of Treviso, at the centre of the plain, which was an important and strongly defended outpost of the Austro-Hungarian line. (The reduction in the flow of the Piave in the decades following the Great War has left the river a shadow of the multi-channelled force that once swept past the island, which is now scarcely an island at all.) This was followed by a second attack some thirteen miles (20km) to the north, directed at the town of Vittorio Veneto, the main target. The Italian Commander-in-Chief, General Armando Diaz, realized that Vittorio Veneto was the key to victory. Its capture would separate the two fronts and cut off the enemy's forces in the mountains to the west, so that they could be 'rolled up' at leisure.

As we shall see, four days later, Harry's battalion joined the attack.

Harry arrived back from leave prior to the start of the offensive. He reports in a letter to Jack that 'they were just coming out of the trenches [on the Asiago Plateau] when I returned.' The battalion was relieved in the line on 26 September, and the war diary takes up the story:

A contemporary illustration from an Italian weekly newspaper, giving a somewhat idealized view of Italian forces in action during the Allied offensive against the Austro-Hungarians that began in October 1918.

26th The Battalion was relieved by the 2nd Battalion, 49th Italian Regiment and a portion of the 2nd Battalion, 50th Italian Regiment, and on relief, moved to SERONA camp.

27th The Battalion moved [south] *by motor lorries from SERONA camp to BEREGANA camp near THIENE, arriving in latter camp at 12 noon.*

On the following day there was a ten-mile (16-km) march almost due south to the next billets.

28th The Battalion moved by march route from BERGANA camp to billets in vicinity of VICENZA, arriving at 11 pm.

29th The Battalion rested during the day. Church services were held in the afternoon. Lt. Col. S.D. Rumbold D.S.O., M.C. took over the temporary command of the 70th Infantry Brigade. Major L. Crampton M.C. took over temporary command of the Battalion.

30th Section & Platoon training was commenced. 'D' Company gave a demonstration – witnessed by the other companies of a 'Company in the Attack' – open warfare.

During the month the health of the battalion was good. The prevailing desease [sic] *was I.C.T.*

(Signed)

L Crampton Major

Commanding 9th Battalion York & Lancaster Regt

> *Oct 1st / 1918*
> *32507/ 9th York & Lancs., C Company,*
> *L.G.S., I.E.F.*

Dear Jack

Just a line to let you know I have arrived safe back in Italy it is not very nice to be after being at home but I shall have to make the best of it. I was very pleased to find them all well at home and Willie looking so well. The weather is still very hot, and we do our marching at night. I hope you got home safe after your holiday. We are on rest at present in Italian barracks but I don't know how long for. Write back soon as possible as it will be a long time before I get a letter.

Remember me to Agnes [Jack's wife].

With best Love to you both.

Harry

The battalion spent two weeks 'resting' – which involved training, route marches, ceremonial drill and cleaning – before marching off for the move to its next location, this time by rail. It is possible that Harry had an inkling of the coming offensive, prompting him to tell Jack that it would be a long time before he would get a letter; however, he may just have been commenting on the length of time it took letters to reach him. At all events, in mid-October the 9th York and Lancasters were on the move again.

> *14th* [October] *The Battalion marched from CORNEDO to THIENE* [10 miles/16km].
> *15th The Battalion entrained at THIENE and detrained at TREVISO occupying billets in the latter town for the night.*

The train journey from Thiene to Treviso covered about forty-five miles (70km) and brought the 9th to within a few miles of the front line on the Piave River.

> *16th The Battalion marched from TREVISO to C HOGARIN near TREVIGNANO* [about ten miles/16km)].
> *17th The Battalion rested during the day. Billets & environs were cleaned.*

Harry took advantage of a day without marching to write to Jack:

> *Oct 17/1918*
> *32507/ 9th York & Lancs., C Company,*
> *L.G.S., 12 Platoon I.E.F.*
>
>   *Dear Jack*
> *I have received your paper and a letter. I am pleased to hear that you are going on alright. We have had some big marches since I came back from leave, it as just about knocked me out, and I don't think we have finished yet, we are still in Italy but on a different front, not far from V.* [see below] *we have never been here before. I have not been in the line yet since I got back, they were just coming out of the trenches when I returned. Last night we stayed a night in a city about as big*

as Nottingham first time we have been in such a big place. There was
plenty of Americans — some had just come out of the line which was
only about 7 kilos so you see it is very quite just now. I expect there
will be something coming off before long. What do you think of the
war do you think it will finish this next summer. Things are dearer up
this end the Italians tells us the farer [farther] *east we get the dearer*
things are. Write as often as you can and send a paper or two, I hope
I see you all again before it is time for another leave.

   With best love to you both from
   Harry
(I am sending a letter for Ethel)

There has been some discussion about the reference to 'V'. I
feel that Harry is almost certainly referring to Venice, less than
twenty miles (32km) south of Treviso, as that is, probably, the only
place in that section of the front of which Jack would have heard.
When he wrote the letter, Harry would have been in Trevignano,
roughly twenty-five miles (40km) north of Venice; the large town
full of American troops must be Treviso.

The men only had one day of rest, the war diary recording
the next move: '18th The Battalion route marched 15 Kilometres:
Men carried full marching order.' Note the distance, equivalent
to about ten miles. Harry and his comrades would have been
carrying well in excess of 65 pounds (30kg). This on the day
after his letter to Jack had reported that the marching 'as just
about knocked me out,' Tough times, but essential fitness training
for the task ahead. Luckily, they were to get another rest on the
following day: '19th Owing to exceptionally wet weather, men
were confined to billets for the day.'

After a few days of toing and froing, marching and shifting
billets, on 26 October they arrived at billets at Catena, within
a couple of miles of the front line on the Piave. Meanwhile, a
few miles away, units of the Italian Army were consolidating
bridgeheads on the north bank of the river. The sounds of artillery
action would have been clearly audible.

'27th, 28th Battalion remained at C. BARCHESSE near

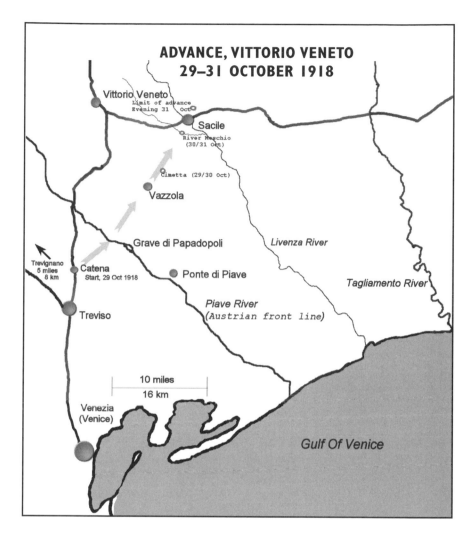

ADVANCE, VITTORIO VENETO
29–31 OCTOBER 1918

Vittorio Veneto
Limit of advance
Evening 31 Oct
Sacile
River Meschio
(30/31 Oct)
Cimetta (29/30 Oct)
Vazzola
Grave di Papadopoli
Livenza River
Trevignano
5 miles
8 km
Catena
Start, 29 Oct 1918
Ponte di Piave
Tagliamento River
Treviso
Piave River
(Austrian front line)

10 miles
16 km

Venezia
(Venice)

Gulf Of Venice

CATENA under orders to move at half-an-hours notice,'
noted the war diary of the next two days. In practice, this
meant that all equipment would be packed, all kit assembled,
ready to move. All the officers would have been briefed by
the CO and they would have briefed their NCOs and men in
turn. The officers had also been sent to reconnoitre the front
line at its nearest point, Palazzon.

NOTHING is to be written on this side except the date and signature of the sender. Sentences not required may be erased. If anything else is added the post card will be destroyed.

[Postage must be prepaid on any letter or post card addressed to the sender of this card.]

I am quite well.

~~I have been admitted into hospital.~~

{ ~~sick~~ } and am going on well.

{ ~~wounded~~ } ~~and hope to be discharged soon.~~

~~I am being sent down to the base.~~

I have received your { letter dated _____

{ telegram ,, _____

{ parcel ,, _____

Letter follows at first opportunity.

~~I have received no letter from you~~

{ ~~lately.~~

{ ~~for a long time.~~

Signature only } *W. H. Lamin*

Date 27/6/18

(B22277.) Wt. 1566—R1619. 6,000/00. 11/17. S. & S .Ltd. E. 1416.

The 'Field Service Post Card' Harry sent to Jack; the other side was used for the address.

Knowing that they would be in action soon, the men would be excited, if a little apprehensive. The last time the 9th Battalion had been involved in a significant advance was at Messines Ridge over sixteen months ago, on a very different battlefield. Harry had the opportunity to fill in a 'Field Service Post Card', a pre-printed card on which the sender deleted lines – such as 'I am quite well' – that were not applicable and added his name and other details, and his signature, but no personal message. It was just enough to let Jack know that he was, at that time, 'alright'.

A couple of days later, Harry had a chance to write a letter, probably early that morning.

29/10/1918
32507/9th Y & Lancs., 12 Platoon, LGS/IEF

Dear Jack

Just a line to let you know that I am going on alright at present and hope to remain so. I have received your papers and was very pleased with them. They seem to be getting on with the war now and I hope it will soon be over [the Germany Army was being driven back all along the Western Front]. *We have been in an Italian town for a day or two the biggest we have been in yet. It is a bit more like war out here at present, but I hope it turns out a success, and the Austrians retire. I think they want peace bad. I hope you are both keeping in good health and I hope the war is finished before it is time for me to have another leave* [in other words, in not much under a year]. *Write as often as you can and let me know how you are getting on.*

With best Love to you both

Harry

Whether Harry has definite knowledge of the Austrians' morale, whether he is drawing his own conclusions or whether the troops have been briefed in order to prepare them for the attack, we

Following the Allies' successful crossing of the Piave, British troops and transport mules cross one of the river's channels on a pontoon bridge erected by engineers. From a watercolour by a war artist who was present.

can't tell. That morning the battalion would have marched the few miles to the river in order to cross at its allotted time, nine o'clock. There is now a motorway over the river close to their crossing point, but then a series of pontoon bridges would have been in place on the Piave, which was swollen from the recent rain. Vazzola (Vassola in the war diary) lies about ten miles (16km) from the starting point. Another mile (1.6km) and they reached the Montecano River, where they encountered some enemy activity, catching up with the lead battalion, which had been slowed by enemy action.

By the end of that first day their advance had reached Cimetta, about eleven miles (18km) from the start point. The front line had been pushed back seven and a half miles (12km) in a single day. Harry's battalion, heading east, passed about ten miles south of Vittorio Veneto, the town from which the battle was to get its name, and the objective that formed the key to General Diaz's plan. The battalion war diary adds a little detail to the description of the day's events:

29th The Battalion crossed the PIAVE at 0900 hours and commenced the advance towards VASSOLA. On reaching the MONTICANO the Battalion moved forwards to support the 8th Battalion Yorkshire Regiment who were held up by hostile shelling & M G fire. Later in the day the Battalion captured the village of CIMETTA and established a line of posts forward of the CAMPO–CEVARO– BGO [Borgo] di SOPRA road [today designated the SP15]. About 150 prisoners, 10 machine guns and 2 small field guns were captured. Our casualties numbered only 31.

All in all, a successful day – especially when compared with some of the advances on the Western Front in 1916 and 1917. The battalion had a good haul of prisoners and equipment, suffering few casualties and making a considerable amount of ground.

Despite the threat of a counter-attack, the next day was quieter:

British infantrymen with captured Austro-Hungarian troops, at least one of whom looks extremely pleased to be out of the fighting. The 9th York and Lancasters took more than 500 prisoners during the final actions of the Italian campaign.

30th The objective for the Battalion was SACILE. On reaching the ORSAGO–SACILE road at point 47, information was received from the cavalry who were then in SACILE that the enemy had counter-attacked and were advancing towards ORSAGO. This Battalion held the Western bank of the river MESCHIO astride the main road, and the bridge-head at point K65. As the enemy counter- attack did not develop, the Battalion took up a defensive position for the night, manning the western side of the river on the southern side of the ORSAGO– SACILE road. Patrols were sent out towards SACILE during the night.

7 prisoners, 2 small field guns and 8 machine guns were captured. There were no casualties in the Battalion during the day.

The Orsago-Sacile road is today designated the SS13. If the battalion had proceeded on the same course, it would have met this road about two miles (3km) to the west of their objective, Sacile. The River Meschio enables us, for once, to pinpoint accurately the battalion's position for the night.

> *31st At 10.00 hours the Battalion advanced towards SACILE. By 12.30 hours we had established a line along the western bank of the LIVENZA but were unable to cross to the eastern side as the bridge had been destroyed and enemy machine-guns in the church steeple, also snipers in houses, kept up incessant fire. After a bombardment of houses etc. by 6" Newton Mortars, Stokes Mortars* [respectively, 6–inch medium and 3-inch trench mortars] *and Machine Guns, the section of 18 pounders* [field guns] *obtained three hits on the church steeple, and no further trouble was caused by hostile machine guns. The pioneers then prepared a bridge over which Companies crossed the LIVENZA – almost in darkness, and by 19.00 hours our objective had been gained: an outpost line was immediately established on the whole front, touch being obtained on either front.*

Austro-Hungarian field guns, machine guns and other weapons captured by Harry's battalion in the last days of the campaign.

It had been another successful day. The remaining resistance in Sacile had been overcome. The River Livenza is quite substantial there, and was in flood, flowing either side of the two islands on which the main part of the town stands. It would have proved a significant obstacle once the bridge had been blown. Maintaining 'touch' is an important military principle: in action, it is essential that each unit links up with the units on each of its flanks so that there is a continuous defensive line.

The 9th Battalion ended the month well, having taken the objectives set for it. The summary by the CO (Lieutenant-Colonel Rumbold, who has clearly returned from having been temporarily in command of a brigade) is statistically impressive:

Total Number of Prisoners captured during operations 298
Wounded & Sick Prisoners in Hospitals 239
Grand Total 537
Total of Field Guns captured............................ 42
..” ..” Machine..........”........... 53
..” ..” Trench Mortars..”...................................... 44
..” ..” Rifles..............”....................................3000

Total number of casualties:–
* Killed..8*
* Wounded...33*

During this month, the health of the Battalion was good, prevailing deseases being:– I.C.T.
(Signed) S D Rumbold
Lieutenant-Colonel
Commanding 9th Battalion York & Lancaster Regiment

A casualty list of eight killed and thirty-three wounded was a modest price to pay in the light of what the battalion had achieved, especially by the standards of that war. Except, of course, that casualties are not ciphers, but lives ended or, very often, ruined, leaving loved ones to mourn or grieve.

On the following day the positions were consolidated beyond Sacile, and the enemy simply melted away.

As November opened, the success of the offensive was all too apparent, although the war diary entries are brief and businesslike:

1st [November] *The Battalion occupied a line of posts in the N.E. outskirts of SACILE. The Austrians were reported to be retiring across the TAGLIAMENTO* [a river some twenty miles (32km) to the east].

2nd The battalion moved by march route to RORAI near PORCIA arriving in billets at 1730 hrs.

The march on 2 November was around five miles (8km) to the west, following the enemy. And then, on the 3rd, the atmosphere changed completely. Clearly, the intelligence reports about the enemy retiring had been confirmed. On that Sunday, it appears that the war has been forgotten, as the deliberations among the high commands and governments of all the combatants filter down to battalion level:

3rd Church Services were held in the morning. Football was played in the afternoon.
4th The armistice with Austria came into force at 15.00 hrs. Billets and environs were improved. A Battalion Concert was held in the evening.

And with that understated, typically undramatic entry, the war diary of the 9th (Service) Battalion, the York and Lancaster Regiment, recorded the end of all fighting on the Italian Front.

That day, Harry wrote to Jack, evidently unaware of the armistice. He gives a good description of the recent successful action, reflecting accurately the accounts in the war diary.

Nov 4th 1918
32507/9th Y & Lancs., C Coy, 12 Platoon

Dear Jack

Just a few lines to hoping you are keeping fit. I am alright at present, but we have had some trying times as you must have seen by the papers what a big success we have had in Italy. Our div is 23rd there are three brigades in it two went and crossed the Piave and two days after we had to releive them and take up a two Brigades front they had advance about 10 kilos [6 miles] we had to take a place called Sacile which was about 30 kilos [19 miles] farther on. We were not long before we found the Austrians first day it was all open fighting a great deal of machine gun fire but not much shelling as he was retiring very quick it was a rum job going through maize fields and searching old houses. of course we could not do anything at night only put sentries out and wait till morning. next day we went to with [within] about four kilos of Sacile without seeing anything and day after we had to take the town of course he had blown the bridge up but we took it before night. We had four wounded in our platoon bullet wounds. The Austrians then retired to the Taglemento [river]. I hope the war is finished by the time you get this letter. My Pal is safe. Kitchens address. 5 Beta Villa, Mayfield Street. He is alright.

Love to you Both
Harry

British infantry – and an Italian boy – on the Asiago Plateau after news of the victory at Vittorio Veneto.

In all of Harry's surviving letters from the Great War, this is the first in which he mentions any of his comrades by name. I have always found it quite astonishing that, in general, soldiers on active service seem to avoid mentioning their comrades in letters, even though friendships formed in battle were intense and enduring. I suspect that soldiers like Harry were aware that reporting friends as casualties would cause anxieties back at home.

The Austro-Hungarian Army, and indeed the entire Austro-Hungarian Empire, had disintegrated in the preceding few days, until an armistice became inevitable, as well as necessary if further suffering were to be avoided. Recording this, the war diary's entry includes a simple, matter-of-fact statement about an event that was of immense and life-changing importance to the men of the battalion. No triumphant hyperbole, not even a metaphorical sigh of relief, just a bald record of the fact. I wonder how the men were told, and what their reaction was.

It is hard to believe, too, that with the fighting over the first thing the men have to do is clean up their billets. (Actually, it is not hard to believe, having myself spent some time in the British Army.)

There may have been serious worries at this point that, having completed the job in Italy, the British, French and American forces there would be transported back to France and Belgium to support the war effort against the German Army. With hindsight, it is obvious that, with only a week to go until the armistice on the Western Front, there would not have been enough time. But, of course, the soldiers wouldn't have known that.

In little over a month after returning from leave, Harry had taken part in the last significant battle on the Italian front. The Battle of Vittorio Veneto had finally completed the destruction of the Austro-Hungarian Army that had become inevitable after the failure of its June offensive. The fighting in Italy was over, and it was to be only days before the war on the Western Front would end and Harry could start to plan for his return home.

CHAPTER 11

ITALY – THE WAR IS OVER

THERE WAS LITTLE IMMEDIATE acknowledgement that the fighting had finished. The war had another week to run on the Western Front, and so it was not yet time for great celebrations. And, of course, this was merely an armistice, an agreement to cease fighting. There was no guarantee, at that time, of permanent peace.

The battalion CO would also be aware that he had several hundred men under his command who needed to be supervised and controlled. Military discipline still had to prevail. (There are stories of how, when the armistice was signed on the Western Front, some units were 'ordered' to celebrate. There were real problems with severe alcohol poisoning, and troops incapable of any rational behaviour for days.)

The war diary records that, for the 9th York and Lancasters, the routine continued much as before the armistice, mimicking the activities of the previous periods of training. There was, however, the introduction of 'recreational training' and quite a bit more football, so perhaps the pressure was not too intense. Yet the men still spent time on route marches, drill, parades and inspections. Even so, with the war finally over, the soldiers – or those who were not Regulars, at least – must have expected to be allowed to go home to get on with their lives as soon as possible. Unfortunately, the process wasn't quite as straightforward as they must have hoped.

The war diary's entry for the day after the armistice with Austria is anodyne even by its standards: '5th & 6th [November] Recreational training was carried out in the morning. Football was played in the afternoon.' Four days later there was a ceremonial return across the Piave with various top brass in attendance: '10th The battalion moved by march route to VASCON. The Corps Commander, Divisional and Brigade Commanders witnessed the recrossing of the PIAVE from the Bridge-head near PALAZZON.'

This was followed, a couple of days later, by a sixty-five-mile (104-km) rail journey to the west, away from the old front line. The training routine continued.

17th Brigade Church Service near RONCHE, being a special thanksgiving service for victory, conducted by the Rev T. F. James C.J. 23rd [a Saturday] *General holiday for the Battalion. A 'victory' dinner was provided for the men. Football was played during the morning, and a concert held in the evening.*

At last, twelve days after Germany signed an armistice on 11 November, here is some acknowledgment that there was something to celebrate. Harry seems to have enjoyed the dinner, as he makes clear in his next letters.

Nov 26th 1918

9th York & Lancs., C Coy 12 Platoon

Dear Kate

I was very pleased to receive a letter from you. I am sending this with Jacks so I hope you get it alright. I was very glad to hear that they are all going on well at Ilkeston, and to hear such a good report about Connie send me her address, so that I can send a card to her. We are in a very poor place cant get anything and nothing to see only hills its about time we got to a town or to England, but I dont suppose we shall get there just yet. I don't suppose I shall be able to get home for some months yet. It will not be so bad if we can get to England. We had a bit of a rough time last time we were in action just at the finish we had to take a town called Sacile the Austrians had blown the bridge up over the river and held us up for five or six hours, but I and [am] *glad to say that I got out of it alright. I hope you have a Merry Xmas it will make a lot of difference now the war is over. I hope you get home for Christmas. Let me know all about Connie if you go to see her anytime and how she is get on with walking. We had a dinner party last week it was called the victory dinner it was very nice. The weather is very cold but it is healthy very cold at night. We are at the bottom of the hills, there is plenty of snow on the top. Write as often as you can and let me know all*

the news you can, I got the papers alright.
  With best love
  Harry

Nov 26 / 1918
Y & Lancs., C Coy 12 Platoon

  Dear Jack
I was very pleased to receive a letter from you. I hope you are
both keeping in good health, as I am in the pink at present. I have
had a letter from Ethel and they are all going on alright. I hope you
received the letter I sent in the green envelope. I sent it to Ilkeston. I
am sending a letter to Kate will you post it for me. The weather as
been very cold just lately. We had a big dinner last week. It was the
victory dinner and alright too. I sent kitchens address in the last letter,
I have forget it but I will get to know, if you have not received it. I am
short of a pipe could you get me one as soon as possible as they are
very dear out here. Has Kate been to see you yet I expect she will be
coming before long. We are having plenty of sports just now running
and football matches but we are in an out of the way place we cant get
anything and there is nothing to see. It is about time they took us to
a town or brought us to England. I hear they are going to break up
the 10th Army on the 10th December, so we might get all parted and
reorganised. I don't suppose I shall get away for some months yet, but
it will not be so bad if we can get to England. Things are very quite
out here just now. I am very pleased that it is all over and we have
finished with the trenches and mountain climbing. Write as often as
you can and let me know how you are going on.
  With best love to you both
  Harry
  E Kitchens address 5 Beta Villas, Mayfield Street, Spring bank, Hull

From the content, especially of his letter to Kate, it looks as
though these are the first letters that Harry has written to Jack
and Kate since the armistice. The home of his friend 'E Kitchen'
would be local to Jack, who was living and working in Hull.
Once again, Harry has sent a green envelope, meaning that its

contents would not be censored locally, and so could be used for any personal or potentially embarrassing remarks. Even so, there is rarely anything in Harry's letters that would have much troubled a military censor.

The month ended with more training, and more of the ordinary tasks that make up so much of an infantryman's life, as the war diary duly noted.

> *27th* [November] *Two Companies practised an advance to-wards an objective (open warfare). The remaining companies were allotted baths.*
> *30th Billets and environs were cleaned during the day. The Commanding officer inspected Companies and Detachments.*

Harry's battalion spent the end of November and December in four locations close to Vicenza, in the foothills of the mountains, some twenty-five miles (40km) south of the Asiago Plateau. 'Educational' lectures by officers started, but still the military training continued. Harry sent only one letter to Jack that month, and that a fairly brief one:

> *Dec 6th 1918*
> *9th Y & L, C Coy, 12 Platoon*
>
> *Dear Jack*
> *Just a line to let you know that I have received your long letter and papers. I am very glad that you visited Kitchen's and found hem alright. He is a decent chap very quite. I hope you got the letter I sent you asking for a pipe as I have broke mine. Ethel tells me what a rum chap Willie was you cant help but laugh when you hear about him. I shall be glad when I see you all again and I hope it will not be long. I am sending you a Christmas card. I hope you get it alright.*
> *Wishing you both a Happy Christmas and New Year.*
> *Harry*

Two days before Christmas, the war diary briefly notes what must have been a fairly momentous event for the battalion:

THE CHURCH ARMY.

ON ACTIVE SERVICE
WITH THE
ITALIAN EXPEDITIONARY FORCE

Dec 6th 1918

Dear Jack

Just a line to let you know
that I have received your long letter and
papers. I am very glad that you
visited Kitchens and found them alright, he
is a decent chap very quiet, I hope you got
the letter I sent you doting for a pipe as
I have broke mine, Ethel told me what
a rum chap Willie was you cant help
but laugh when you hear about him
I shall be glad when I see you all again
and I hope it will not be long I am sending
you a Christmas card. I hope you get it alright
Wishing you both a Happy Christmas &
New Year

Harry

Like the YMCA, the Church Army
provided facilities for British troops on active service.

23 [December]. *Range Practices. 1st Stage of Rifle Meeting. First Dispersal Draft of 55 other ranks left the Battalion for the Concentration Camp at 'Tavernelle'.*

Here was some sign that troops were, at last, heading for home. A small number, but a start. 'Concentration Camp' has chilling connotations for the modern reader, but here it should be taken literally – a camp where the soldiers for dispersal were gathered together. (Tavernelle is some two miles [3km] south-west of Vicenza.)

If Harry recorded anything else of the last month of 1918, the year in which the Great War finally ended, it has not survived. He is clearly longing to be demobilized and allowed to go home; however, he is enough of a realist to recognize that in his case this is unlikely to happen very soon.

For Harry, the great event of January 1919 was a trip he made with an unspecified number of his comrades to Venice. We can work out that it must have been on the weekend of 25 and 26 January. He complained in his letters that he was short of money, and was then given £5 back pay to take on his leave. Today, that £5 is worth around £250, and so he could afford to stay in 'The Grand Canal Hotel' – no doubt an improvement on his billet. He had a few worries about spending all the money but, sensibly, realized that he would never get another chance for such a visit. As long as he was 'on the right side' – that is, not in debt – he was happy.

For those who have never visited Venice, we now have television, magazines, websites and films that provide a good idea of the wonders of the city. To Harry in 1919, however, the canals, St Mark's Square, the churches, must have been nothing short of astonishing. Before his trip, his letters to Jack and Kate show that he is beginning to concern himself with matters beyond the narrow military world in which he had lived for the past two years.

> *32507/9th Batt york & Lancs*
> *C. Coy 12 Platoon., I.E.F, Italy*
> *Jan 2/1/1919*

Dear Jack,

I am sending you a few lines just to let you know that I am alright and keeping in good health. It is a long time since [I] had a letter from you, but I got the pipe alright which you sent. I am glad that you and Agnes are keeping well, and I hope you have had a happy Christmas although I expect you have both been very busy Christmas was very quite out here, but I enjoyed myself in a way, not much money but we had a good dinner. We are in a little town called Arzignano [about 15 miles/24km west of Vicenza] it is a very damp place as it lies in a valley between the mountains. I dont know when I shall get home but I hope it will not be long. All men going on leave now are alright for if they get work while at home they can stop so it makes it better for them. About all the miners have gone, some which came up in April 1918 [i.e. long after Harry joined the battalion] have got away. Let me know next time you write if you got the cards I sent. I am glad to hear that they are all keeping well at home and are keeping free of the flu. I guess you must have a busy time in Hull with so many prisoners of the war coming in. Everything is so dear out hear the money now is thirty lires to a pound, we used to get forty at one time but still things are no cheaper rather dearer Willie must be getting a rum chap as Ethel tells me some funny tales about him in her letters. Write as often as you can and let me know all the news, I hope soon to be able to write you from England. Wishing you both A Happy New Year

　　With best Love to you both

　　Harry

It would appear that if soldiers on leave manage to find work, they can apply to quit the Army and take up the job. Jack was a priest in Hull, a major port, and he may well have ministered to returning prisoners of war who landed there.

32507/9th Y&L., C.Coy., I.E.F
Jan 22/1919

　　Dear Kate

I have just received your letter and was very pleased with it, it was such a long time since I heard from you. I am glad that Connie is getting on alright I hope she will soon be able to walk. I have not wrote to the firm [his former employer] yet I think it is not much use, as I dont think they have much work. Ethel has not said anything about the other men writing I dont think they all have if they want us they ought to send for us. I am going on as well as possible but I am just about fed up. Well I think we all are its about time we all got home but I expect we shall have to wait a bit and be patience things are very dear out here and I am very short of money as we dont get much pay Glad to hear that you　enjoyed you holiday with Jack and to hear that he is getting on

alright. Write as often as you can and let me know all the news. If you
can spare a shilling [£0.05 – about £2.50 today] *I should be very*
pleased as it would come in alright, hoping to see you soon
    With Best Love
    Harry

Of course, in early February his letters are full of the trip to Venice.
Thereafter they turn to the work he is doing and, inevitably, to
demobilization. There is no great optimism yet about getting home.
He might have got his discharge from the Army if he had had a job
to go to (he mentions a 'slip' which would have been a job offer)
but, clearly, Truman's lace factory in Ilkeston, where he had worked
before the war, was not taking on workers. The latter years of the
war had seen a remarkable change in employment patterns. With
so many men in uniform, young women had started to work in
factories, enjoying the status and the wages, which were significantly
better than could possibly have been earned in domestic service –
for many women the only real employment open to them before
the war. They would not be keen to give up their factory jobs.

During the month he got a new job with the Church Army,
a very British version of the YMCA that provided facilities for
off-duty troops – as well as good food for the novice cook. He
uses Church Army headed notepaper for several of his letters, and
presumably worked there after he had completed his military duties
for the day. Then, after his experiences of catering in the Church
Army, he moved on to a new job cooking in the Officers' Mess
at Divisional Headquarters. He feels the job is 'no good for a man
who as ad two years in the trenches without a break,' perhaps the
first trace of bitterness he has shown in the whole of his war service.
I can't begrudge him that, just as he can be forgiven for forgetting
that he had in fact had one two-week leave in September 1918.

Back on form again, Harry is making the best of the job, asking
for help with the cooking. As to the reference he makes to 'two and
three months leave', some soldiers were given a long leave which
they could use to find civilian work, and so 'earn' demobilization.

Dear Jack

Just a line to let you know I am alright I have not much time as I am very busy man this week I have been working in the Church Army dishing tea out in the afternoon and night. I dont get away till 9.30 p.m so I have not much time the job is alright, but I expect we [i.e. the battalion] are moving next week so I shall have to go back to the company, but address my letters the same as I get them alright We have a parson in charge of us of course he is like all the rest a bit of an old figgett [fidget?] gets excited now and again, so you have to talk to him a bit. We have had supper with him these last four nights, of course we have cooked it between us. Well before I had this job I had a weekend at Venice, about three days, It is a most wonderful city, all built on small islands and their is some fine buildings. I went in S. Marks Church it is a wonderful sight, well I enjoyed my self very much, I got £5.00 to go with so I expect I shall be debt now but that does not matter so long that I am on the right side, and I thought I shall never get another chance. I will tell you all about it when I see you I hope to be seeing you in the summer time. Well write as often as you can I am pleased to hear that you and Agnes are keeping well. I hope you will write as often as you can. I am very pleased that they are going on alright at Ilkeston, Ethel tells me what a rum chap Willie gets I shall be glad to get home again I would rather do any thing than go on parade and do guards in fact I think I would rather be in the trenches in Italy. I am just going to have supper now.

With best love to you both
Harry

[undated – probably written at the same time as the letter to Jack above]

32507/9th Batt

Dear Kate

I am getting on alright and am sorry I ask you to send me a shilling or two as the next day I was given a week end leave. I got £5.00 and went to Venice it is one of the most wonderfulest cities in Italy, it must be a sight in summer time to see the boats on the river and canals We put up at the Grand Canal Hotel, and we was alright. I have bought Connie and

Willie a broach and Ethel a present, things are very dear, but I did not mind, and I had a shilling or two left. I will tell you all about it when I get home but I dont know when that will be, I hope it will not be long, only men with slips are getting home and I dont think our firm have got any work so they not bother with slips. I am glad that they are going on well at home, and pleased to hear about Connie I hope she will be able to walk soon I am working in the Church army Hut this week so I dont require any money, the job is all right plenty to eat, so you bet I dont grumble I have just made supper stewed meat, onions and potatoe and a piece of toast not bad, I dont think I shall be here above a week. I will write again soon but write as often as you can

With Love
Harry

Later that month he writes again, among other things telling his brother and sister that he is now at Divisional HQ:

Feb 28/2/19

Dear Jack
I am sorry that I have not wrote for such a long time but you see I have been all over the shop, I am cooking at present in the officers mess for eight of them, three majors at that I dont know how long I shall be here. I have been here a fortnight, I expect I shall have to leave when they get an experience cook. the only thing I am bottled at [no good at, or confused by] *is pastry. it is all work I have not had a night off yet and dont look like getting one. I am at the Divisional Head Quarters these jobs are alright when there is a war on but no good to a man who as had two years in the trenches without a break. you see the cook as got Demob. I hope you got my letter telling you about my visit to Venice I am very pleased I went. I dont know when I shall get demobed I might have to go* [to Germany] *with the army of occupation, but I expect I shall be out of the army some time this year. I am very glad that they are going on alright at Ilkeston and that Willie and Connie is well. if you dont here from me you must write as I am so busy at present I get seven lires a week extra that is about 5/-* [5 shillings – £0.25] *English money. of course I live well, you can bet on that. but there is*

such a lot of work. Well the next time I write I might have another
job, or they might keep me. I will let you know as we are expecting
breaking the division up any time the address at present is

>   *23 D.H.Q, C Mess, I.E.F.*
>   *Remember me to Agnes with best love*
>   *Harry*

>   *Dear Kate*

I have received your postal order alright, but I could have managed
alright. I have left the Church Army so I have finished making tea
I liked it alright. But you see the Batt moved to another place so
I had to go with them. I have got another job now I am helping
to cook at the Divisional Head Quarters mess but I dont know
how to make fancy thing but you know I liked cooking, I should
be very pleased if you would send me a small cookery book, it
might be useful, but you see we cant get all the things we want,
we have to make pies and pastry with self rising flour, you might
give me a few wrinkles [hints or tips] *how to go on how to make*
small meat savours [savouries] *and a few sweets and so forth I am*
asking you all these things and I might get the sack but not out of
the Army, I wish I could, I hope you received my letter telling you
about me going to Venice, I enjoyed myself very much I am glad
that they are going on alright at home, I shall be glad when I get
there but I think it will be a few months yet there so quite a lot
of our men taking on. I think it is this two & three months leave
that is doing it, but it will take a lot to make me list I have wrote
to Trumans factory but I have not heard from them yet Write as
soon as you can well right away as soon as you get my letter my
address at the present is

>   *32507 Pt Lamin*
>   *23 D.H.Q, C.Mess, I.E.F*
>   *With Best Love*
>   *Harry*

In writing 'it will take a lot to make me list,' Harry is saying that
he is not keen to join the Regular Army. Many soldiers, finding

on demobilization that there were no civilian jobs, re-enlisted.

In March, Harry is writing about 1920 as a date for his demobilization, which is not at all encouraging. Still, he is keeping his job cooking in the Officers' Mess at Divisional HQ. By now the division has moved to Tavernelle, which seems to be the muster point for soldiers beginning the railway journey home. Willie has his third birthday on 23 March.

March 12

23. D.H.Q., 9th Batt Y+L., C.Mess., I.E.F., Italy

Dear Kate

Just a line to let you know that I am alright and still cooking but I expect the Division will break up in a week or two. your book came in very useful. I should not like to be without it. Here was four messes on D.H.Q and ours is the only one left. I thought I should have to leave and let on[e] of the other cooks come, but I still keep my place. I should like to be officers servant [also known as a batman or soldier-servant] *when we break up, but I expect I shall be with army of occupation till I get demobed. I dont mean soldiering if I can get a job any how while I am in the army. I hope I am out of it before 1920 any way. Write as often as you can and let me know how you are getting on I will write and let you know how I am getting on and where I get too.*

With Love

Harry

He mentions the Army of Occupation again in his letter to Jack of the same day. Commanded by Plumer until April 1919 and based in Cologne, the presence of the British Army of Occupation on the Rhine was a condition of the peace treaty that was eventually signed in June that year.

23. D.H.Q., C.Mess., I.E.F., Italy

March 12

Dear Jack

Just a line to let you know that I am alright and still working. our mess is the only one left we keep getting fresh officers but I still keep my place as cook. I expect the division will break up in a week or two. I dont know were I shall get to. I shall try hard for officers servant when we break up

*but I expect I shall be with the army occupation for a while. but I dont
mind so much as long that I am employed I have had my share of guards
etc. I have received your tobacco alright and was very pleased with it. I am
lucky to be here till now as all the cooks from the other three messes have
finished I thought they would take me place, but I keep as clean as possible
I think that as a lot to do with it not the cooking but its a big job as you
always messing with the fire. We have had the General for dinner but I got
on alright. mind you I dont cook any poultry or game. Write Every week
and let me know how you are both getting on*

> *With Best Love to you Both*
> *Harry*

In April, after Harry has got to grips with his cooking duties – quite
successfully, it seems – the Officers' Mess is broken up and he moves
to a new location further to the west, and a new job guarding an
ammunition dump. The different jobs he's been doing have caused
him to be separated from the rest of his battalion, a significant parting
of ways, given that he has spent nearly two years, through some hard
and often dangerous times, with these men. At least his finances seem
to be sound, his back pay accumulating the equivalent in today's
money of around £450.

In his letters that April, Harry talks about Fiume (which he spells
'Fuime'), to which the rest of the battalion has been sent. With the
breakup of the Austro-Hungarian Empire, this former Austrian port
on the north-eastern Adriatic coast (now Rijeka in Croatia) was
claimed by Italy, along with the nearby ports of Trieste and Pola
(Pula); in 1919 an expedition of Italian volunteers under the poet
and adventurer Gabriele d'Annunzio seized Fiume, which they held
until 1921. Italy maintained its claims on the city and the surrounding
territories but, at this stage of the international deliberations (the
Paris Peace Conference was still in session), seemed to be losing out.
Allied troops were therefore sent to the port to keep the peace and
encourage stability.

April 5/1919

> *Dear Kate*
> *Just a line to let you know that I am alright and in the best of health.*

I had a letter from Ethel she told me you have had your letters returned no wonder they could not find me as I have been all over the shop lately. D.H.Q as broke up and gone to England so have finished working I was the only cook left so I did very well but such a lot of work I had ten officers and more to cook for at the finish to much at it from 6.30 AM to 10.30 PM they must have thought it was a restaurant but I pulled through we had the General with us to finish up with had a big dinner last night seven courses and I got congratulated on it so I was satisfied. I have not drawn a money since January 28 and I got 10/6 [£0.525] bonus from Feb 1st so that is about £9.00 to my credit and I have never had so much money while I have been in the army you see the officers gave us so much a week so I am set up now for a bit, I liked the job but I did not feel so well always being shut up I dont know how I shall get on when I get back to the factory again. I hope I shall be seeing you before long, how is Connie getting on. The weather here is very fine

My address at present is
9th Y+L Regt., G.H.Q Demob, Concentration Camp,
I.E.F Italy
I might get one with a bit of luck but I can quite understand the letters going back as I have been all over the shop lately I am in a little place call Tavernelle in the province of Vicenza near the province of Verona you will see it on the map. I hope you get this letter and I hope I shall be seeing you all before long

With Best Love
Harry

In his letter to Jack of the same date, he expands a little on his disaffection with the Army and the slowness of his progress towards demobilization:

April 5th/1919

Dear Jack
Just a line to let you know that I am alright and in good health I am not at Fuime but a small place called Tavernelle in the province of Vicenza it is next province to Verona. All the lads from our batt as gone to Fuime. I finished cooking two or three days ago when the D.HQ

broke up. Ours was the only mess left and we had BGD general Beaman [Brigadier-General A. B. Beauman, commanding 69 Brigade] *with us the last few days so we had some big dinners all the officers thought me and the waiter was on the D.H.Q cadre and was going with them to England they were surprised we had to stop had they known we should have gone with them but it does not matter we should have been soldiers in England when I come home I want to get demobed. There is to much work cooking for officers 6.30 AM till 10.30 PM to much if I can get out I shall. We had ten officers and more sometimes to look after not bad I had a big dinner last night and got congratulated on it by all the officers and one or two had their wives with them so I was satisfied although I had a lot of work. Remember me to Agnes. If there are any more leave trains to Rome or Naples I shall try my best to get on one as I shall never get the chance again. I hope I do not have to go to Fuime I dont want any more guards or sloping arms* [a rifle drill] *as I am fed up with that I would rather be up the mountains again. when do you think peace will be signed, cooking as been a good thing for me as I have not drawn any money since January 29 and I get the 10/6 bonus from Feb 1st so that is over £9.00 to my credit. My address at present is*

    32507 PT Lamin

    9th Y+L C of G.H.Q, Concentration Camp, I.E.F, Italy

You can send a letter here I might get it with a bit of luck and I might not as I dont think we shall be here long

    With Best Love to you both

    Harry

Of a letter to Kate three days later, only the first page survives. It carries momentous news, however, told with Harry's typical matter-of-factness:

                                     April 8th 1919

    Dear Kate

Just a line to let you know I am alright I am still in Italy at a small village called Rivalto it is very nearly in France it is alright I have finished cooking for a bit it is nice to get out D.H.Q broke up and all officers went to England so I was let behind my Batt had gone to

After nearly two years with the 9th York and Lancasters, Harry transfers to a different regiment, the Royal Munster Fusiliers.

Fuime in Austria what was left of them. I am now attached to the Royal Munster Fusiliers it is an Irish Regt they wear the shamrock behind the cap badge. I have not changed my badge. I still . . . [the rest of the letter is missing]

The Royal Munster Fusiliers (RMF) was disbanded, with a number of other Irish regiments, in 1922, after the establishment of the Irish Free State (now the Republic of Ireland) as a country independent of the United Kingdom. The 1st (Garrison) Battalion, RMF, to which Harry has been attached, served in Italy from January 1918 to April 1920, based at Arquata Scriva, about twenty miles (32km) south-east of Alessandria, in Piedmont. Harry's next letter, to Jack nearly three weeks later, makes no reference to his change of regiment, other than the initials 'RMF' in his address.

32507 9th Y+L

attached R.M.F., A.P.O [Army Post Office],

L. 1 Box R, Italy

April 26/19

Dear Jack

Just a line to let you know that I am alright and in good health I have not had any letters for about six weeks now. but I have been moving about a lot I hope I am settled down now till they send me home for good send me a paper or two regular if you can. I have seen no news for a long time. The weather here as been very nice lately. we are in a little country place about like Strelly [Strelley, a small Nottinghamshire village just east of Ilkeston] *guarding ammunition etc. there is only about forty of us all together but there is a lot of Italians guarding it too. I hope Agnes is keeping well and all at home. I hope to get a letter from you soon. I expect Willie is getting quite a man now he is turned three expect I am for army of occupation as I have got my 10/6 bonus. How is things going on in England and what do you think about the Fuime job and America.*

Write soon With Best Love to you both
Harry

British troops were still in Fiume – where d'Annunzio was effectively establishing himself as a dictator – largely to keep the peace between the Italians and the local population. The reference to America may come from the stance of US President Woodrow Wilson at the Paris Peace Conference, who was markedly determined not to see the German people punished too harshly by the peace terms, in contrast to the attitude of, in particular, the French. Wilson was also determined to establish a 'League of Nations', as a means of ensuring that such a war could never again take place. Harry appears to have sent only one letter – or only one that survives – in May, and he does not seem to have been able to write to Jack again that month.

Dear Jack

Just a line to let you know that I have received your letter. We are in a out of the way place just now, if you have an old shirt or a towel will you send it on as soon as possible as it is very hard to get changes up here there is about 40 of us guarding a dump it consists of all sorts guns etc. Write as soon as you can and let me know all the news. I am please that you and Agnes are keeping in good health. If you have got an old shirt send it on as soon as possible. my address is at present.

> *32507, 9th Y+L, attached R.M.F, A.P.O.,*
> *L. 1 Box R, I.E.F, Italy*

With Best love to you both Harry
I will write again in a day or two and tell you a bit more.

In June, however, he is able to write at greater length. As always with requests to Jack or Kate, Harry's request for a shirt has been swiftly answered:

> *32507/9th Y+L, attached R.M.F,*
> *A.P.O. Box R., L. 1 I.E.F, Italy*
> *June 1st/1919*

Dear Jack

I have received the shirt alright it is very nice. but I have not got the towel yet I am sure it is very good of you to be so much trouble. but my shirt is in half it has been a job to get exchanges were we are but I think we shall get some before long. I am very pleased that you and Agnes are keeping in good health. and I hop you enjoy your holidays. the weather hear is very hot. We are at a small country place about like Cossall [a hamlet a mile east of Ilkeston] *it is very pleasant there is only about forty infantry men here altogether. I think we are all being transfered to the Munsters that is not very nice as the Munsters have been here all the time we have been in Italy they were all old men and B1 or 2* [Army fitness grades, A1 being the highest] *you see they never went in the line but just did garrision duty about fifty miles behind the line but I dont care as long as I get home alright. Write and tell me as soon as you see anything about demob in the papers as we can get to know nothing about it out here. I have had a letter telling me that Annie is getting married. I hope she will be happy. I dont know what Ethel and Willie will do I am sure as it means giving the house up at Whitworth Rd. I am pleased to hear that you are thinking of getting a better job soon I hope you get to a nice place it will be alright. Write as often as you can I am getting letters pretty regular now.*

With Best Love to you both Harry

P.S It would be nice for Willie to pay you a visit if you were near Ilkeston I am sure he would enjoy himself.

June 22/19

    Dear Jack

Just a line to let you know that I have received your letter and the towel you sent it is very good of you to sent it. Ethel and Annie wants me to try and get home on leave for August, but its no use me asking from this end there is some men here now with 18 months in without leave although they are going on leave from Fuime with eight months if they write for leave they want to send to the war office as it is no use at all sending here any way I hope to be home on leave by October as I think it will get down to twelve months when peace is signed let me know as soon as that happens as we dont here much out here. I am still officers servant and cook but I dont know out long it will last. Do you think you could send Ethel 10/- [10 shillings – £0.50] a month and begin in the first week in July and then the first week in August till I get a leave and then I might draw some credits [against his Army pay]. No doubt they will ask you to write for a special leave if you do write to the war office ask I should like to get home when things break up, any way let me know what you think best. Write as often as you can and let me know all the news, do you think the Germans will sign peace, if they do we should be demobed in six months time. I shall be very pleased to get out of it although I have not done any drilling now for about six months and I have always had eggs and bacon for breakfast while I have been a this country place and plenty of new potatoes and fruit I was surprised at the Derby winner [the unfancied Grand Parade, which came home at 33-1; the Derby was run at Newmarket from 1915 to 1918, but returned to Epsom in 1919]. I will write a line to Mrs Higgins when I have time and tell her that I did not receive her parcel which she sent at christmas. Are you going home for Annie wedding she told me in her last letter that she had wrote and ask you, let me know if you do, Ethel tells me that they have given notice at Whitworth Rd. I dont think it will be very healthy for Willie at Mill street. I hope she gets another house. Write as often as you can hoping you and Agnes are keeping in the best of health.

    With Best Love
    Harry

On 28 June 1919 the Treaty of Versailles was signed, finally ending the war with Germany (there were different treaties for each of the enemy combatant nations: Hungary signed its on 4 June 1919, Austria on 10 September, Bulgaria on 27 November and Turkey on 10 August 1920, although the latter was never ratified). I was always a little confused to find that one of Harry's medals indicated that the Great War lasted from 1914 to 1919, when everyone knew that the fighting finished in November 1918. But of course the various

The French Marshal Ferdinand Foch (second from right), C-in-C of the Allied forces on the Western Front, with other members of the Allied delegation that signed the armistice with Germany on 11 November 1918 – so ending the fighting, and thus the war.

armistices only marked the end of offensive operations, whereas the treaties formalized the end of the war, and were signed by all the combatant nations.

There are only two surviving letters from July, and Harry is still no nearer being demobilized. The weather would be very hot by now, so sleeping in the open air wouldn't be a great hardship. His sister Sarah Anne (Annie) is getting married, and so that is a point of interest. Jack has clearly written, perhaps to Divisional HQ, or to the battalion, about Harry, and this seems to have caused some problems. The family would want him home for Annie's wedding, I imagine, but he is certain that the military authorities will take no notice; he has already told Jack not to send any more such letters.

It might be helpful to clear things up about the family addresses: so far as I can tell, Ethel and Willie are living with Annie at Whitworth Road in Ilkeston, although Harry and Ethel's main home is in Mill Street (Whitworth Road is about a mile from Mill Street, and was then a little more upmarket). Connie, still not walking properly, is at a boarding school in Liverpool, Jack and his wife are still in Hull, and Kate in Leeds.

Harry's question about 'thousands listing' is interesting. Work is short and some ex-soldiers, finding the transition to civilian life difficult, are re-enlisting into the forces. That apart, he is fit and well, but seems to be concerned with the finer things of life, asking Kate for handkerchiefs and hair cream (pomade, which he spells 'Pomard', was a popular dressing for men's hair). He has managed to get the job he wanted, officers' servant, and perhaps wants to smarten up.

> *32507/ 9th Y+L attach Royal Munsters Fusiliers.,*
> *A.P.O. Box R, L 1., I.E.F Italy*
> *July 1*

> *Dear Kate*
> *Just a few lines to let you know that I am alright and in good health I dont think I shall get leave yet a while well I am sure not, there are so many men with 18 months without a leave, I expect one before Christmas anyway now that peace is signed I hope it will not be long before we are all at home I am still doing officers servant and cooking*

and we are still sleeping in the open field so we get plenty of fresh air night and day I am pleased to hear that they are all going on alright at home, and I should like to know if Connie can walk yet she will soon have been their a year now it is a long time I am glad to hear that Willie is keeping well and all at home. I hope Annie will be alright when married well I think she will be. Write as often as you can and let me know all the news and if you hear anything about demob in the papers Jack as wrote [i.e. has written] *to the office out hear about leave and* [I] *told him in my last letter not to do so as it was no use to write hear at all. I have never got the papers you were going to send and yesterday I got two of your letters together. Write as often as you can and let me know all the news and when Annie is getting married.*

With Best Love

Harry

P.S I would be very pleased if you could send me a few cheap handkercheifs as I have not got any at all and also a tin of Pomard.

32507/9th Y+L attached Royal Munster Fusiliers
A.P.O. Box R. L.1., I.E.F, Italy
July 1

Dear Jack

Just a line to let you know that I am alright and keeping in good health. The officer here as just had a letter from you asking him about leave, as I told you in my letter it is not a bit of good writing here as there is so many men with 18 month in without leave dont write here again whatever you do for I shall be surprised if I hear anything about leave for another four months at least anyway now peace is signed I hope we shall all be home for good before long. I am still doing officers servant and cooking for him but I dont know how long it will last, I think I have kept the job well I think I told you in my last letter that about a dozen of us were sleeping in a field in the open so we have plenty of fresh air night and day we have been [sleeping] *out now for about five or six weeks. Do you think you will be able to get home for Annie wedding, I hope she will be alright I hope you enough* [enjoy?] *yourselves in the country it will be a nice change for both of you. Write as often as you can land let me know how you are getting on and if you see anything about*

Demob in the papers its about time they started about it. Is it true that there are thousands listing [enlisting] *every week in England again. I have had a letter from home and I am pleased to say that they are all getting on well could you allow Ethel 10/- a month of the money and begin the first week in July if so let me know. I will write again soon*

    With Best Love to you Both

    Harry

From August to December 1919, Harry's letters paint a picture of a man anxious to quit the Army and go home at last, but resigned to his fate, only too well aware of how slowly military bureaucracy can move.

August 6/1919

32507/9th Y+L attached Royal Munster Fusiliers

A.P.O. Box R. L.9, I.E.F. Italy

    Dear Jack

I was very pleased to received your letter. And to hear that you had a good time when on your holidays. I dont think I should bother any more now about writing as I expect I shall get a leave before September [is?] *out I might get one any time now, as I have nearly twelve months in* [since his last leave], *and it is a long time to go without leave especially when then war is over. I expect I shall get out of the army about next spring if all goes well. All the men who joined up before July 1st 1916 are getting released from the army as soon as possible, so I expect when this lot is gone I shall be amongst the next. If I hear anything about a leave I will write and let you know as soon as possible. I am very pleased you paid a visit to Ilkeston and found them well but I hope Annie's face is better. I guess Will gets a rum chap what had he got to say to you Ethel tells me he gets no better always up to some tricks. he was going to send me a parcel last time Ethel wrote all sorts of things bobbins etc. The weather hear is very hot. I think it is the hottest month of the year. I expect we shall be out of Italy by november. so if that is correct I shall have had two years in Italy quite long enough. Write as often as you can and let me know all the news. I will write again soon.*

    With Best Love to you both

    Harry   *(P.S) Address same only L.9 instead of L.1*

32507/ 9th Batt Y+L attached Royal Munsters Fusiliers
A.P.O. Box R. L9 I.E.F. Italy
Aug 8/8/19

Dear Kate

I have received your letter and was very pleased with it. I have also had a letter from Jack. I have told him not to bother now as I expect coming home on leave next month perhaps before. It is very hot out here this month and we are still out in the country, but I dont get much time off. Write and tell me how Annie is getting on I have not had a letter for a long [time]. *I had a letter from Ethel telling me she had gone back to Mill street but both are keeping in good health Willie must get a rum chap as he is always up to some tricks I shall be glad to get home again but trade is very slack. I think I shall manage to get out of the army by about April next year. it might be before, well I hope so. Let me know what Annie said about Connie and if she is keeping in good health. If I hear any thing about leave I will let you know at once. Jack told me in his last letter that he enjoyed his holidays very much and that he found time to visit Ilkeston. Did you get the letter about me asking for one or two cheap handkerchiefs. Write as often as you can, but if you have not sent any handkerchiefs I should not bother* [to send them now].

With Best Love

Harry   *(PS) Address same only L9, instead of L1*

32507/9th Batt Y+L att Royal Munster Fusiler
A.P.O. Box R. L9.,I.E.F Italy
August 19th/1919

Dear Kate

Just a line to let you know that I have received your letter, I have also received one from Jack. Ethel told me in her last letter that Annie had got married I am very glad that it is all over. I think she will be alright. I was pleased to hear that Mr Leverton was their and Annie Bonser [a relation of Harry's mother]. *I dont know when I shall get a leave but I hope it will not be long, write as often as you can and let me know all the news. It has been very hot this month out hear. We dont get to know much about demob I expect they will soon start now write as often as you can*

With Best Love

Harry

Aug 23rd

Dear Kate

Just a line to let you know that I have received your letter. I am pleased to hear that the wedding came off alright and that it is all over. It as been awful hot out hear this month and we have had no rain for a long time. The grapes are just about getting ripe, well in another weeks time they will be getting them. I hope to be on leave very soon as it will very soon be a year since I was at home. so I think it is time I had one I will let you know as soon as I hear anything about it. I am pleased to hear that they are all keeping well at home. I have been transfered to the Munster Fusiliers now so my proper address and No will be at the bottom of the letter. Write as often as you can and let me know how you are getting on. What did Annie think to Connie when she went to see her does she get any better. I will write again soon

With Best Love

Harry

Address

40843 Pt Lamin, 1st Gar [Garrison] *Batt*

Royal Munster Fusiliers

A.P.O. Box R L9

I.E.F. Italy

Harry's permanent transfer to the Royal Munster Fusiliers means that he has been allotted a new regimental number.

40843, 1st Gar. Batt., Royal Munster Fusiliers

A.P.O. Box R. L9, I.E.F. Italy

Aug 23rd

Dear Jack

Just a line to let you known that I am alright and keeping well. I have heard nothing about leave yet but I hope to be home in September sometime, if I have good luck. I am very pleased to know that you found Ethel and Willie well. I have been transferred to the Munsters

altogether now, so I have got a fresh No. It as been awful hot out here
this month. we have hardly known what to do. The grapes are just
about to ripe I expect in another week or so they will be getting them.
I am pleased to hear that Annie wedding came off alright and I hope
she will be happy. I expect Willie will miss her for a bit but they will
have to make the best of it.

    With Best Love to you both
    Harry

August turned to September, but whatever Harry's hopes for
leave, they were not rewarded.

      40843 / 1st Garr Batt., Royal Munster Fusiliers,
      A. P.O Box R L9, I.E.F. Italy
      Sept 10th

    Dear Jack
Just a line to let you know that I have received your paper and letter.
The explosion you speak of was at the dump we are guarding but it
was nothing. it might have been worse I think one Austrian prisoner
got killed of course biggest part of the men here belong to A.O.G and
have seen no fighting at all so it would be terrible to them. I dont
know when I shall get on leave now as it is stopped for September
expect for special leave when a man goes on leave from here he does
not return but stops in England. You can please yourself whether you
write for a special leave but whattever you do dont write to this end. if
you could not get any thing from the war office dont write here I would
rather wait six months I expect I shall be home for Christmas. Write
as often as you can and let me know all the news. Glad to here that
you are both keeping in good health. Ethel address is 19 Mill Street.
I think it is all this time I will write again soon.

    with Best Love to you both
    Harry
If you write for leave tell them that I have only just been transferred
to the 1st G RMF as this Batt as seen no fighting at all. It is twelve
months now since last leave.

Harry's PS seems to indicate that he is anxious for the authorities

Aug 23rd   40843.

> 1st Gar. Batt
> Royal Munster Fusiliers
> A.P.O. Box R. L 9
> I.E.F. Italy

Dear Jack

Just a line to let you known that I am alright and keeping well I have heard nothing about leave yet but I hope to the home in September sometime, if I have good luck. I am very pleased to know that you found Ethel and Willie well. I have been transfered to the Munsters altogether now, so I have got a fresh No. It as been awful hot out here this month. we have hardly known what to do. The grapes are just about ripe I expect in another week or so they will be getting them. I am pleased to hear that Annie wedding come off alright and I hope she will be happy, I expect Willie will miss her for a bit, but they will have to make the best of it.

With Best Love to you both Harry

Harry's letter to Jack, showing his new regimental number.

to know that he has seen action, unlike the 1st Garrison Battalion of the Munsters, which had been sent to Italy to provide guards for headquarters, ammunition dumps, airfields, and so. On through October and November, into December, and still Harry has no leave, and no news of his demobilization.

1st Garr Batt., Royal Munster Fusiliers,
A.P.O Box R L9, I.E.F. Italy

Dear Jack

I have received your letter alright and I am very pleased to hear that you are going on alright. I think it is a good job that you got the furniture before the railway strike [in Britain, September to October 1919] *came off as you might have lost it altogether. I don't think it is hardly worth while writing now, but you see it is a long while without leave thirteen months, and the war finished as they have been going at six months from Fuime out of the Y & L. I have seen some of them on the train at a place called Alexandra* [Alessandria, a city and province in Piedmont, north-west Italy; the city lies about forty miles (64km) south-south-west of Milan]. *I went down for a day's outing there and they were just going back off leave, they tell me what a fine place it is. There is a big do on at Rome next week and some of the R Cs* [Roman Catholics] *have got a chance to go for 7 days. I wish I belonged to the R.C. I might have had a chance I should have liked to have seen Rome before I left Italy. I hope to be out of this country before November is out and I might stand a chance of getting demobilised before Christmas. I would be satisfied then. anyway we shall have to wait and see as leave as been stopped here to let the men get home that jioned* [sic] *up before 1st July 1916. I think they have plenty of work at Trumans now but I don't know whether I shall go back or not. It will not be very nice at first being shut up after being out in the fresh air for about 3 years. Well theres one good thing to be thankful for The place I visit is the chief place in the province of Alexandra and about as big as Nottingham. Write as often as you can.*

With Best Love to you both
Harry

Harry is a little unhappy about leaving the rest of the 9th York and Lancasters. In his own way, he is complaining that while he hasn't had a leave for thirteen months, some of his battalion have had a leave after only six months' service.

One of Harry's envelopes to Kate, showing the censor's stamp.

Oct 9/19

40843/1st Garr Batt., Royal Munster Fusiliers,

A.P.O Box R L9, I.E.F. Italy

Dear Kate

Just a line to let you know that I am getting on alright, but have heard nothing yet about leave. There are some men with two or three months in more than I have got [i.e. have served for two or three months longer than Harry] *but I hope to be home before Christmas. I was very pleased to hear that Connie was getting on alright and to hear that she was very happy. I should like to hear of her walking. I mean paying her a visit the first chance I get. If I hear anything about coming home I will write and let you know. I have just wrote to Annie its the first time I have wrote since she was married. I hope it finds her alright. It is now nearly fourteen months since I was home so I think it is about time I got home if it was only for a leave. Ethel tells me they are doing better a*[t] *Trumans so thats a good sign of more work. Write and let me know how you are getting on. All the men who came up before 1st July have gone home except one or two and they are going home next week so it looks a lot better. Will write again soon.*

With Best Love

Harry

Oct 24/1919
40843/1st Garr Batt., Royal Munster Fusiliers,
A.P.O Box R L9 I.E.F., Italy

Dear Jack

I have just received your letter and was very pleased with it. I am glad to hear that you and Agnes are keeping in the best of health, as I am in the pink only this last day or two I have had the tooth ache but I think it is a cold. I have had a letter from Ethel and they are all keeping well at Ilkeston. You ask me if I was cooking. No I have finished cooking and am doing guards and escorting Austrian prisoners but I can do it. I could have had a job yesterday cooking for two officers but I am not having it. never finished till 10 o clock at night and up about 7. you have no time for anything cant get out at all and they think no more about you when you have done it. of course the foods all good but in the camp were we are we live well. you can buy eggs and get all sorts of tin stuff from the canteen so we don't do amiss. I hope to get home before Christmas if not on demob I hope to get a leave it will be three years come Christmas. Dec 28th since I joined up. I don't know when we are moving out of this country but I hope it will be soon. i will let you know if I hear any thing. They keep getting rumours about that we are moving but they never come off. Write and let me know all the news send a newspaper next time you write.

With Best love to you both
Harry

Oct 30/10/19
40843/1st Garr Batt., Royal Munster Fusiliers,
A.P.O Box R L9, I.E.F. Italy

Dear Kate

I was very pleased to receive a letter from you and to hear that you are keeping in good health. I am sorry that Connie does not get on with her walking but we shall have to make the best of it. I have wrote to Annie so I expect I shall get a letter before long. There is no signs of me getting demobilised yet as there is some men here yet that come up here in April 1916. If I could get a leave, I could easily get demobed when I got to England but the thing is getting there as there is no leave going from here, only odd ones they are only men for demobilisation, but any way I hope to be home for Christmas. Write as often as you can and let me know all the news. I had a letter from Ethel and she said that Willie as had a cold but he is a lot better now. I hope he keeps in good health. The weather hear is very cold at night but the sun gets out well during the day. I will write and let you know if I hear anything about getting home.

    With best Love

    Harry

Nov 18

40843 / Royal Munster Fusiliers,

A.P.O Box L1 D Coy., I.E.F. Italy

    Dear Jack,

Just a line to let you know that I am in good health, but am wanting to get home, and there seems no sign of it yet. the last train from here went 5 or 6 weeks ago. goodness knows when the next is going. It is over fourteen months since my last leave and I belong to the 1916 men, but in December. Young lads are getting home, 1918 men, on compassionate grounds. I would be glad if you would try and get me a leave by writing to the war office. dont write hear as it would be of no use, as only special leaves are going, if you write do it at once as we might be moving any time. I think I have earned a leave as it was 17 months before I got my first leave. I have been moved from the village Rivalto and I am now at a place called Auquato [Arquata Scrivia]. Let me know if you write to the war office. I am pleased to hear that they are all keeping well at Ilkeston and to hear that Annie is keeping well, but they all want to know when I am going to come home as all the other chaps as got out of the army who joined up when I did. Write back as soon as possible as it is a long time since I had a letter. Hoping that this letter finds you all in the best of health.

    With Best Love to all

    Harry

    address now 1st Garrison

    40843 / Royal Munster Fusiliers

    A. P.O. L1

    IEF Italy

December 11/1919

Dear Jack

Just a line to let you know that I am alright and in good health. I don't think it is any good writing about getting home as their is no chance of getting home for Christmas it looks like being more like the middle of April before I get home. I might manage it a bit before. all the prisoners are going home this month so it will make it a bit better after Christmas for us all. I am very pleased to here that all are going on alright at home & keeping in good health. I hope you and Agnes have a Happy Christmas & New Year. I am sorry that I shall not be at home for it but I am in good health so that is something. Write as often as you can and let me know all the news and send me a newspaper or two. I will write again soon.

With Best Love to you both

Harry

40843/1st Garr Batt, Royal Munster Fusiliers,
D. Coy. 17 Hut, A.P.O. L9 IEF, Italy

It is now exactly a year and a month since the armistice with Germany came into effect. The year 1919 is drawing to an end, and yet still there is no real sign of any progress towards Harry going home. When the fighting on the Italian Front ceased over a year ago, he would surely have expected to be back with his family before long.

He has also been very unfortunate with leave. I had assumed that he had been granted leave in the summer of 1917, but from his letters it's clear that he went from his leave at the end of basic training, in the spring of 1917, right through to September 1918, without any other time away. Now he has completed another fifteen months without a break. So much for the entitlement of two weeks' leave a year. If he had stayed with the 9th York and Lancasters, it seems that he would, at the least, have been granted leave by now.

CHAPTER 12

HOMEWARD BOUND

CHRISTMAS 1919 HAS JUST PASSED. As far as I have been able to work out, Harry is at a base a few miles to the south of Tortona, in the province of Alessandria, where he has been for some time.

On 27 December he writes this postcard to Jack, postmarked the 28th:

Dec 27/1919

Dear Jack

Just a line to let you know that I have received the tin of tobacco. I was very pleased with it. Do not write again till you here from me as I am moving from this place on the 29 Dec. will send post card as soon as possible.

Harry

While it isn't clear from the card, leaving Tortona will be the first step in his journey home. At last . . .

Three days later, on the first day of the new year, he writes to

Kate and to Jack from Marseilles, this time with definite news of his demobilization.

Jan 1st 1920

Dear Kate

Just a line to let you know that I have left Italy and have arrived in France at Marseilles. I dont think we shall be here more than a day or two. we got in today at 4 o clock. and we are not allowed out of camp so I expect we shall have to stay in. I hope to be in England this time next week that is with good luck. I have got my papers for demobilisation so I expect to get demobilised within this next fortnight so I hope to be seeing you before long. I hope you had a Merry Xmas and a Happy New Year and I hope Connie enjoyed her holiday. I will write and let you know as soon as possible how I get on.

With Best Love
Harry

Jan 1st 1920

Dear Jack

Just a line to let you know that I have left Italy. I am at present at Marseilles how long I am here for I do not know but I don't think it will be more than a day or two. We have just got here by train and we are not allowed in the place so I expect we shall have to stay in camp. We was on the train about twenty eight hours so we went well for a troop train. I received your tobacco alright it was very good. I hope you have both had a Merry Xmas. I expect you have been very busy. It is very cold here and wet I don't know what it is like in England I expect to be there within another weeks time with a bit of luck. I will write and let you know if I am so you need not bother writing till you hear from me.

With Best Love to you both
Harry

The journey by rail from Italy to Marseilles would have been rather less than 250 miles (400km), so the speed was about normal for a troop train, averaging a little less than 10 miles an hour.

Five days later, Harry sends another postcard to Jack, this time from one of the YMCA establishments that were still providing facilities for troops serving abroad.

POST CARD

Jan 6/1920

Dear Jack

Just a line to let you know that I am alright. We have left Marseilles after having three days their. We were allowed out its a fine big city and you meet all sorts of people. At present I am in Calais and hope to be in England by Thursday at Ripon if good luck. Hope to be seeing you soon.

With Love Harry

Nearly home! I would think that his most likely means of travel would have been by train from Marseilles, retracing in reverse most of the route he had taken with the battalion in November 1917. The YMCA has put its own postmark on the card; Harry must have stayed in Hut 2.

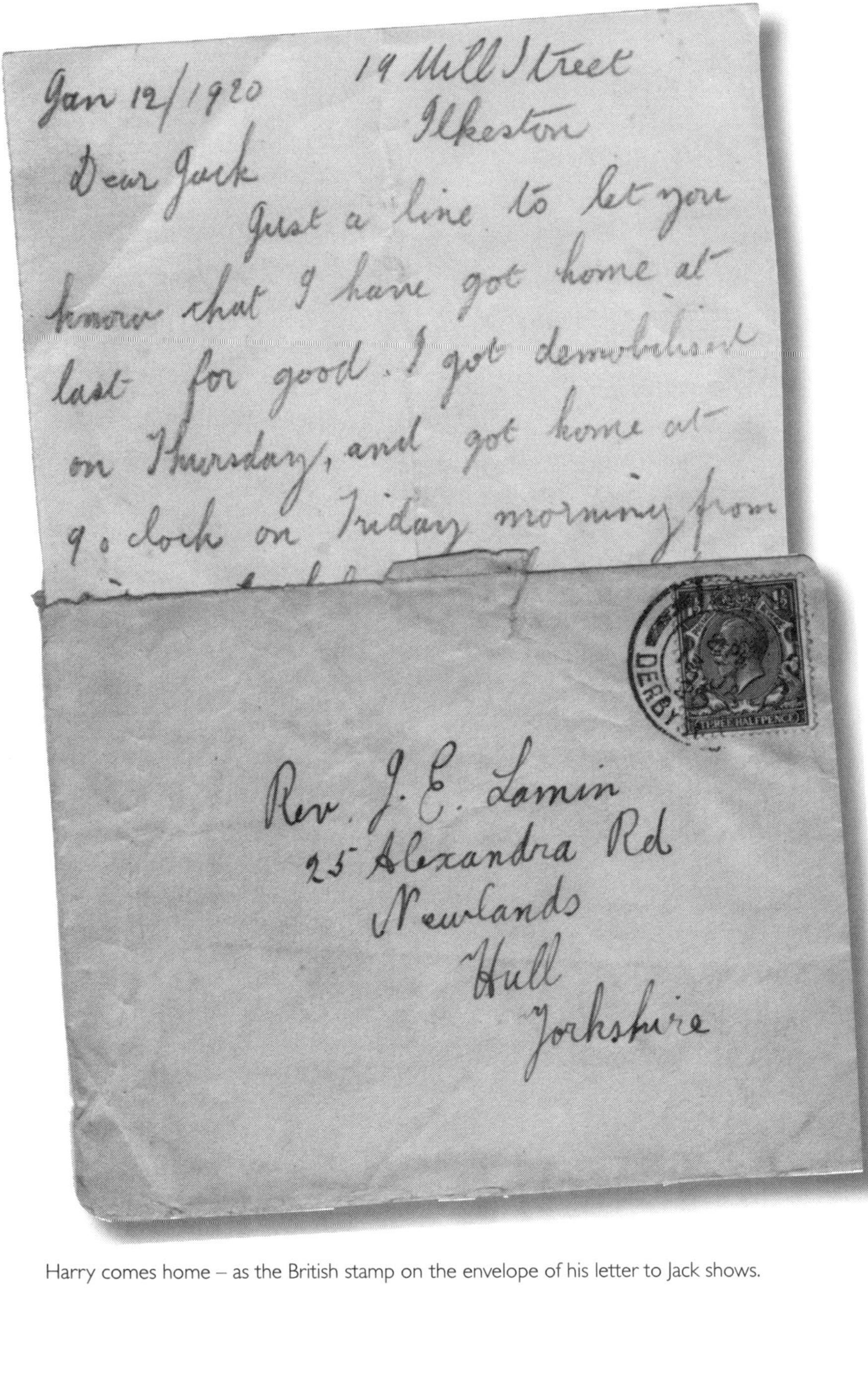

Jan 12/1920

19 Mill Street
Ilkeston

Dear Jack

Just a line to let you know that I have got home at last for good. I got demobilised on Thursday, and got home at 9 o'clock on Friday morning from

Rev. J. E. Lamin
25 Alexandra Rd
Newlands
Hull
Yorkshire

Harry comes home – as the British stamp on the envelope of his letter to Jack shows.

Finally, we come to the letter that signifies the end of the war for Private Harry Lamin.

> *Jan 12th/ 1920*
> *19 Mill Street, Ilkeston*

> *Dear Jack*
>
> *Just a line to let you know that I have got home at last for good. I got demobilised on Thursday, and got home at 9 o clock on Friday morning from Ripon. Ethel thanks you for the 10/- you sent. We are all in good health except for me I have just a bit of a sore throat but I hope it is well in a day or two. the weather is very wet just now. I dont know whether I shall start at Trumans or not, they seem to be quite busy just now. I will write again soon and let you know what I am going to do.*
>
> *With best Love to you both*
> *Harry*

POSTSCRIPT

IT IS DIFFICULT TO WRITE the last chapter of this book. Ironically, it was relatively easy to chart the part of Harry's life when he was in the Army. The course of his life and the events in it were indicated by his letters and the battalion's war diary and, with a bit of detective work, it was quite possible to produce a reasonably full account.

For the period after the war had ended, however, I found that there was virtually no documentation available. I am in the situation in which many have found themselves as the years have passed: it is simply too late to ask, as there is no one left who knew Harry well. Sadly 'Willie', my father, no longer has a reliable memory, and so cannot really contribute much. I am left with the long-ago childhood memories of my sister Anita and myself, as well as any official documents that I can find, to paint some sort of picture of the remaining forty years of Harry's life.

We have seen that he returned to the family home in Mill Street, Ilkeston. He left the Army with £61 2s 1d (£61.10), a substantial sum in 1920. It sounds rather less impressive, however, on recalling the three years of military service that he endured. In today's terms it is worth about £3,000, so it was by no means a fortune. The final sum includes the back pay that he was owed of £33 19s 3d (£33.96; worth about £1,700 today) and a 'War gratuity' of the princely sum of £15 (£750). He also received four weeks' leave, paid at 4s a day (£0.20, worth £10 today!), an allowance for rations and a clothing allowance of £2 12s 6d (£2.62), worth today around £130. And that was it. After three years in uniform, often in conditions of unimaginable hardship, danger and terror, the total payment to Harry came to about £3,000 at today's values.

The £1 'deduction for overcoat' shown on the certificate meant that Harry was allowed to keep his Army greatcoat for the journey home. If he were to hand it in to the local railway station, he would be reimbursed the £1 – about £50 today. The rest of his pay settlement was made in instalments, the final payment being made on 29 January 1920.

The official Army form notifying Harry of the pay due to him. It is not known whether he handed in the overcoat and reclaimed the £1 deposit.

Later, in the 1940s, Harry and Ethel moved from Mill Street to nearby Gordon Street, where they lived for the rest of their lives. There is a family legend that Harry could not accept the idea of moving house, even to a much pleasanter home, and so Ethel arranged the move one day while he was at work. He came home to find the job done.

Harry (in a dark suit, third from right in the second row) at Willie's wedding in 1941; his older brother Jack, who officiated, is in the centre of the back row. Nancy sits in the centre of the front row with Willie behind her and her mother-in-law, Ethel, on her left. Kate, looking 'formidable', is second from left in the front row, and Annie is at far right. The photograph therefore brings together all the principal characters in this account except Connie.

A precious photograph shows Harry at Willie's wedding to Nancy, my mother, in 1941. Modest to the last, he was the sort of man who tended to disappear when photographs were being taken, so very few survive.

As children, Anita and I would sometimes stay for weekends with our grandparents at Gordon Street. I remember those visits with great affection. Harry was working in a lace factory in Derby, travelling the ten miles or so to and from work by bus.

He was a quiet man. I can recall walking with him to the nearby gasworks with a wheelbarrow to pick up coke for the fire, perfectly companionably, but neither of us saying much. He would sometimes go for a day out to the races at Southwell, near Nottingham. At that time, the only legal way to gamble on horses was to use the on-course bookmakers, and my sister tells me that Ethel did not approve of his gambling. Apart from that, he was, apparently, very reluctant to go away from home, even for day trips, never mind for a holiday. Perhaps this was a product of his war experiences, but Anita recalls a more unhappy legacy. She remembers him sleeping in an armchair after Sunday lunch and waking screaming. 'It's the war,' Grandma Ethel explained.

Connie died in 1929, aged nineteen, from complications following an operation – all linked to the cerebral palsy with which she had been afflicted as a baby. She was buried on Christmas Eve in the large municipal cemetery in Ilkeston. Having raised her as their own, one can imagine what a tragedy this must have been for Harry and Ethel, as well as Kate – Harry's letters from the war often mention Connie in the fondest terms, and he is always solicitous of her welfare. Kate herself died in 1948 at the age of seventy-one, and was buried with the daughter whom she had never been able to acknowledge in life. Brother Jack died in 1945, aged seventy-five, a distinguished clergyman; I am told that there is a plaque to him in York Minster.

There is one other familiar name to account for. Like so many other units raised after August 1914, the 9th (Service) Battalion, the York and Lancaster Regiment was disbanded after the end of the Great War, as the hugely swollen armed services shrank back to peacetime levels. The regiment went on to raise more battalions for the Second World War, including a new 9th Battalion, and these too disappeared after that war ended in 1945. The regiment was disbanded in 1968 (although maintaining its regimental headquarters until 1987), so ending the history of a distinguished infantry formation whose two original components, the 65th and 84th Regiments of Foot, had begun life in 1758 and 1793, respectively. Of the men who served in the twenty-two battalions of the regiment that

Harry (back row, far right) and Ethel (directly in front of him), probably taken towards the end of the 1950s, when Harry would have been in his late sixties or early seventies. This is the last known photograph of him.

fought in the Great War, 8,814 were killed or died of wounds. Between them they won 1,190 awards for gallantry, including four Victoria Crosses.

The only other photograph of Harry that I have been able to find would appear to have been taken at a family gathering, or perhaps a social-club outing. My guess is that it dates from the late 1950s.

Harry retired at sixty-five in 1952, and lived until 1961, when he died peacefully at home. My mother, telling me of his death, reported that he said, 'I've had a good life.'

GLOSSARY

APO – Army Post Office; also known as a field post office

Bde – brigade; also 'bgde'. A British infantry brigade in the Great War usually consisted of four infantry battalions, one of which often served as a Pioneer (q.v.) battalion, plus a machine-gun company (heavy – i.e. Vickers [q.v.] – machine guns) and a trench-mortar battery. The 9th York and Lancasters formed part of 70 Brigade, with the 11th Sherwood Foresters, the 8th King's Own Yorkshire Light Infantry (KOYLI) and the 8th York and Lancasters; from October 1915 until February 1916 the brigade also included a Territorial battalion of the Middlesex Regiment. *See also* Division

BEF – British Expeditionary Force, the name generally used to refer to the British military forces – including Dominion and Imperial units – on the Western Front, 1914–18, and especially to the initial (small, by comparison to the French and German armies) force of two corps (q.v.) that arrived in France in August 1914. In fact there were several BEFs – e.g. in Palestine and other theatres – including the BEF Italy, the title first given to the British force of five divisions under General Plumer that was sent to Italy in November 1917, to assist the Italian forces after their heavy defeat at Caporetto in October. The title was changed to 'Italian Expeditionary Force' early in 1918, to reflect the involvement of the French and Americans in the Italian campaign

Bn – battalion; also written as 'batt' or 'battn'. British regiments in 1914 consisted of at least two Regular battalions, at least one Reserve battalion and at least one and usually several more Territorial battalions. Under the various recruitment schemes instituted by Field Marshal Lord Kitchener, the Secretary of State for War, in August 1914, regiments raised many more battalions for the conflict, known as 'New Army' battalions and given the designation '(Service)' in the battalion title; the 9th York and Lancasters was a New Army or Service battalion. A British infantry battalion of the Great War had a nominal strength of 30 officers and 977 other ranks (**see** OR), but on active service the effect of casualties often reduced battalions to far smaller numbers. Commanded by a lieutenant-colonel, each battalion comprised a battalion headquarters and four companies (**see** Coy).

Bomb, bomber – in the Great War, 'bomb' was often used to denote a hand grenade; 'bombers' were soldiers selected to attack the enemy with grenades. *See also* Mills bomb, P bomb, Rifle bomber.

Bully, bully beef – tinned corned beef, from French *bouillé*, boiled. A staple of British soldiers throughout the Great War

C–in–C – commander-in-chief, the overall commander of a military force or forces in a theatre or sector of war.

CO – commanding officer, also referred to as OC (*see below*). Usually a lieutenant-colonel, but because of casualties battalions sometimes ended up under the temporary command of a major, or even a captain.

Corps – Originally 'Army Corps', a military unit usually consisting of two divisions (q.v.) plus attached troops forming a sub-division of an army. The BEF in France and Belgium, initially just two corps, grew so large that it was divided into five armies (First, Second, Third, Fourth and Reserve, later renamed Fifth Army), each with its own corps; there were also a Cavalry Corps, an Indian Corps, a Canadian Corps, and an Australian and New Zealand Army Corps, the famous ANZACs. The word can be misleading, as the

British Army applies it to other formations: the Royal Engineers and the Royal Army Medical Corps, among others, are designated 'corps', and at the time of the Great War there was a Machine Gun Corps, a Tank Corps, the Royal Flying Corps, and even an infantry regiment named the King's Royal Rifle Corps. The 23rd Division, which included Harry's battalion in its 70 Brigade, served in X Corps on the Western Front, and in XIV Corps in Italy.

Coy – company, the basic unit of an infantry battalion (**see** Bn). In the Great War, British battalions were generally divided into five companies: a headquarters company (or 'Company Headquarters') and four rifle companies, usually designated 'A', 'B', 'C' and 'D'. Rifle companies were subdivided into four platoons (**see** Pln). Each company was commanded by a major or a captain, with (usually) a captain as second-in-command; there was a company HQ, as well as a company sergeant-major (CSM, q.v.) and a company quartermaster sergeant, and at full strength numbered over 220 officers, warrant officers (q.v.), NCOs and other ranks (**see** OR).

CSM – company sergeant-major; a warrant officer (q.v.), rather than an NCO.

DCM – Distinguished Conduct Medal, a gallantry award for ORs (q.v.) and ranked only one degree below the VC (q.v.).

Div, Divl, Divnl – abbreviations for division (q.v.) or divisional.

Division – military formation usually, in the British Army of the Great War, consisting of three brigades (Bde, q.v.) plus 'divisional troops' – artillery, engineers, mounted troops, medical and transport services, and so on. For the time that Harry was with the battalion, 70 Brigade (which included the 9th York and Lancasters) was part of the 23rd Division, together with 68 and 69 Brigades (for a time between 1915 and 1916, including the Battle of the Somme, 70 Brigade was detached to 8th Division, being replaced for the period by 24 Brigade from that division). The 23rd Division served in X Corps of Plumer's Second Army in Flanders until November 1917, and then transferred to XIV Corps, also of Second Army, on moving to the Italian Front.

DSO – Distinguished Service Order, a decoration for 'meritorious or distinguished service in war' instituted in 1886. Awarded only to officers, it ranks immediately below the VC (q.v.; the equivalent award for other ranks was the DCM, q.v.). It was generally awarded to officers of the rank of major or above, but in exceptional circumstances was occasionally won by more junior officers.

Entrenching tool – a two-piece implement consisting of a short wooden helve and a steel head which fitted on to it. The latter had a small spade-like blade at one end and a short pickaxe head at the other. An invaluable piece of equipment for the infantryman, it was designed in 1908 and was still in service in the Second World War.

GOC – general officer commanding; that is, the general in command of a particular formation, whether a brigade (a brigadier in the Great War was still designated brigadier-general), division, corps or army; thus at Messines in 1917 Plumer was GOC Second Army.

ICT – inflamed connective tissue. Something of a mystery hangs over this acronym, which certainly stands for inflamed connective tissue nowadays. However, that seems to cover a number of ailments like tendonitis, whereas the war diary's several mentions of it would point more to something like trench foot, although there has been a suggestion that it may have been some sort of stomach complaint. I have been unable to find more; perhaps a reader may be able to enlighten me?

IEF – Italian Expeditionary Force. **See** BEF.

Interior economy – From time to time during the Italian campaign, the war diary (q.v.) reports an activity known as 'interior economy'. This was a term used for the day-to-day administration of the battalion in respect of the basic housekeeping of the soldiers. Equipment, clothing and weapons would be cleaned, repaired and inspected to make sure that everything was in order.

Lewis gun – gas-operated, magazine-fed, rifle-calibre automatic weapon with a nominal rate of fire of 500–600 rounds per minute, the standard light machine gun of the British, Dominion and Imperial forces during most of the Great War. Invented by an American, Colonel Isaac Newton Lewis, in 1911, it proved accurate and reliable, and was quickly adopted by the British Army, and tens of thousands were built under licence in the UK. British-built versions were in .303-inch calibre, and US-built ones in .30-inch; there was also a lighter version of the gun, without the cooling barrel shroud, fitted to countless Allied aircraft. There were two versions of the drum magazine, one holding 47 rounds and the other 97 (the infantry tended to use the former). At 28 pounds, the weapon was light enough to be operated by a single gunner, and the folding bipod beneath the barrel added to its accuracy. Many thousand Lewises were dug out of store and refurbished for use in the Second World War, especially as a light anti-aircraft weapon.

LG – Lewis gun (see under 'Lewis' above).

LGS – Lewis-gun section.

MC – Military Cross, a gallantry award introduced in 1914 for commissioned officers of the rank of captain and lower (extended, after the Great War, to include majors) and for warrant officers (q.v.; senior NCOs of the rank of, or equivalent to, sergeant-major). As a decoration for officers (it is nowadays awarded to all ranks) it ranked third below the VC and the DSO (qq.v.).

Mills bomb – the standard-issue hand grenade of the British Army during most of the Great War, officially designated the No. 5 grenade. It was invented in 1915 by a William Mills, who manufactured the grenades at a munitions factory in Birmingham.

Minenwerfer – German trench mortar (q.v.).

MM – Military Medal, a decoration for gallantry awarded to other ranks (*see* OR); the equivalent for officers was the MC (q.v.).

NCO – non-commissioned officer. In the British Army, subordinate officers, such as lance-corporals, corporals and sergeants, appointed from the ranks, rather than holding a commission from the sovereign, as an officer does, or a warrant, as a warrant officer (q.v.) does.

OC – officer commanding – as in 'OC B Company'.

OR(s) – other rank(s); that is, all soldiers who are not officers, namely warrant officers (WOs), non commissioned officers (NCOs) and privates (qq.v.).

'Pals' battalions – the name often given to certain New Army (*see* Bn) battalions made up from men who had enlisted together in local recruiting campaigns, and who were given a promise that they would be allowed to serve together rather than being split up and sent to already existing battalions. This meant that groups of friends, fellow workers and neighbours from the same areas were able to join up, train and fight together, and in the North Country and Midlands, especially, there was an enthusiastic response to the idea. Many famous units came to be known by their Pals designation, among them the Accrington Pals (11th East Lancashire Regiment), and the Sheffield City Battalion (12th York and Lancaster Regiment). In practice, however, the idea proved something of a disaster, for when these battalions suffered heavy casualties – as they did, notoriously, on the first day of the Battle of the Somme, 1 July 1916 – the effect upon their local communities at home was that these cities and towns suffered disproportionate losses among their young men. Once conscription was introduced in January 1916 no more Pals battalions were raised.

Pass – a signed paper, usually issued by battalion headquarters, permitting a soldier to go on leave for a specified period of time. Should he fail to return by the due date or time, he would be 'absent without leave' (AWOL).

P bomb – a smoke grenade containing a main charge of phosphorus, which gives off a dense white smoke once detonated.

PH helmet – phenate hexamine helmet, an early type of gas mask, consisting of a cloth hood with eyepieces and a valve for exhaling; the permeable cloth was treated with chemicals to neutralize noxious gases, and was reasonably effective against phosgene, chlorine and tear gas.

Pioneer – pioneers are soldiers employed to perform basic construction duties, such as repairs to roads or military railways, work on trenches and other defences, the establishment of barbed-wire entanglements, and so on. In the Great War they were essentially trained infantrymen, often from mining or construction backgrounds, who performed these tasks, to the extent that a number of infantry battalions were converted into Pioneer units, although later in the war specialist Pioneer units were raised.

Pln – platoon. Infantry battalions were divided into companies (**see** Coy), which were sub-divided into platoons, each under a lieutenant or second lieutenant. Platoons were further sub-divided into sections, each under an NCO (q.v.); Harry, for instance, served in the Lewis-Gun Section (or Machine-Gun Section) of No. 12 Platoon, C Company, 9th (Service) Battalion, the York and Lancaster Regiment.

Rifle bombers, rifle grenade – a rifle bomb or rifle grenade is a grenade equipped with a rod that is inserted down a rifle barrel, and then fired at the enemy using a special blank cartridge. They could travel much further than hand-thrown grenades, and were usually more accurate, so several soldiers in any infantry company would be trained in their use.

Pte – private (soldier), the lowest rank of fully trained soldier in the British Army. Not all private soldiers are so called: thus a private in the Royal Artillery is designated Gunner; in the Royal Engineers, Sapper; in a cavalry regiment, Trooper; in a Rifle regiment, Rifleman, and so on.

SBR – small box respirator, a type of gas mask introduced in 1916 to replace the PH helmet (q.v.). It consisted of a rubberized mask with eyepieces and a mouthpiece connected by a hose to the 'box' filter contained in a cloth bag worn on the soldier's chest. More effective than the PH helmet, and easier to use because the filter was separate from the mask, it was much preferred by the soldiers.

Semaphore – a system of signalling with flags (or, if necessary, the arms) using an alphabetic code, each letter signified by the position at which the signaller holds the flag or flags. Semaphore was a vital communication technique in the Great War, being much more reliable than the then primitive radio or field telephones.

Specialists – soldiers who had acquired special skills, among them Lewis gunners, signallers, scouts and bombers (grenade teams). Specialists are referred to several times in the war diary (q.v.).

Trench foot – also called 'immersion foot', a painful and, if untreated, dangerous affliction of the feet caused by long immersion in water, mud or otherwise damp conditions, and made worse by troops being unable to change socks and boots for dry ones. In extreme cases it could lead to amputation. It was extremely common among all the combatants in the Great War, and is still a threat to soldiers on active service; many British servicemen serving in the Falklands campaign of 1982 were to suffer from trench foot, partly due to poor-quality boots.

Trench mortar – a comparatively portable short-range weapon designed to fire an explosive projectile at a high angle, the advantage being that fire then falls into an enemy's trench or other defences. The standard British trench mortar was the 3-inch Stokes, which could fire a high-explosive bomb weighing just under 11 pounds (4.84kg) at ranges of up to 800 yards (730 metres). The German equivalent was the *Minenwerfer*, which was built in a number of calibres, the 77-mm (just under 3 inches) and the 170-mm (6.7-inch) weapons being the ones most commonly deployed in the trenches.

VC – Victoria Cross, the nation's highest decoration 'for valour', instituted in 1856 and awarded to ORs as well as officers.

Very pistol – single-shot, breech-loading flare pistol issued to front-line units, used to fire signal flares, for instance to summon artillery support. The colour of the flare (red, green or white) served as a simple code, red indicating a request for help or support. It was named for its inventor, Edward W. Very, an officer of the US Navy.

Vickers gun – tripod-mounted machine gun based on the Maxim design (Maxims were used by the German and Austro-Hungarian forces, and had originally equipped the battalions forming the BEF [q.v.] at the beginning of the war), the standard heavy machine gun of the British Army from well before the Great War until decades after it. Like the Lewis (q.v.), it was of .303-inch calibre, and fired the standard rifle round, as well as tracer, and had a nominal rate of fire of 450–600 rounds per minute. There the similarity ended, however, for as well as being water-cooled (and much heavier), the Vickers was recoil-operated and fed by a belt holding 250 rounds, rather than a magazine. Vickers guns were operated by two-man crews from companies of the Machine Gun Corps, each infantry brigade (**see** Bde) having such a company attached to it; as with Lewis-gun sections, the gunner and loader were protected by a small team of riflemen. It proved to be one of the most reliable automatic weapons ever made.

War diary – a formal daily record kept by military units from battalion level (or equivalent – e.g. an artillery battery) upwards. The keeping of war diaries was mandatory, and forms were provided for the purpose. In an infantry unit, they were written up at battalion headquarters, although the exigencies of battle sometimes made it impossible for them to be added to daily. The war diaries of British battalions from the Great War, including that of the 9th York and Lancasters, are in many cases held at the National Archives, Kew (http://nationalarchives.gov.uk/).

Warrant – i) *see* warrant officer; ii) 'railway' warrant, a paper issued to soldiers who had to travel anywhere by train, serving in place of a ticket and accepted by all the railway companies, which would then reclaim the cost of tickets from the War Office.

Warrant officer – a non-commissioned officer ranking above an NCO (q.v.) but below a commissioned officer, and so called because of the warrant for their appointment issued to them by the War Office (nowadays by the Ministry of Defence; by contrast, a commissioned officer holds a commission from the sovereign). Abbreviated to WO, there are two grades: WOI (warrant officer class one) – regimental sergeant-majors and equivalent – and WOII – company sergeant-majors and equivalent.

ACKNOWLEDGEMENTS

It is very difficult to complete this section. As Harry's blog progressed and developed into this book, help has been offered from so many directions. Perhaps I can apologize now if I have omitted anyone who feels that they should be here. I know that, as soon as I have closed this section and sent it to press, I'll realize, with horror, that I've left an important contributor out.

I must thank my sister Anita, who has supported me from the start, and who has been able to fill many of the gaps and to point me in the right direction for research into the family background. 'Willie', my father, Bill Lamin Senior, has provided real motivation for the project.

The Internet readers of Harry's blog have, between them, written thousands of inspirational and supportive comments. Without those comments it would have been much more difficult to retain enthusiasm for the task. As well as support, many have provided information and guidance to make it possible for a novice researcher to make some sensible progress.

Of those readers, Jono Wood, Bob Lembke and Rocco Chiarolanza have provided superb supportive material that has helped make sense of Harry's experiences. John Murray took a very battered and tatty, but vitally important, photograph of Harry in uniform – the only one in existence, so far as we know – and worked his magic on it, to restore it to a presentable state.

Especial mention must be made of Joanne Allen for providing help and support as the blog developed and transformed into the book, and to Lucy Cook for making sense of a muddled bundle of letters.

Thanks are also due to Mark of Soverign Tours for organizing a trip that enabled me to retrace Harry's steps through the Flanders battlefields.

In the early days of the blog, members of the History Department at Pool Business and Enterprise College in Cornwall persuaded me that Harry's letters were of value and well worth developing. Andie Parker-Jones, Paul Annear and Jeremy Rowe were so enthusiastic about the project that I had little choice but to proceed. Phil Jones, the Network Manager at the school, was of great help with any technical problems encountered when publishing the blog

The research was an interesting challenge, having little knowledge of the background to the First World War. The National Archives in Kew, formerly the Public Record Office, carries a treasure trove of material, the war diary of Harry's battalion, in particular, proving an invaluable resource. It was especially helpful, living in West Cornwall, that much of this material was available online (http://nationalarchives.gov.uk).

Without the resources available on the Internet, the project would have been much poorer. There is a wealth of websites containing relevant material, and I frequently consulted many of these to confirm information or to get a different view on a topic. (I should add that this is by no means an exhaustive list):

> www.flanders1917.info
> www.1914-1918.net
> www.bbc.co.uk/history/worldwars/wwone
> www.gwpda.org
> www.historylearningsite.co.uk/ww1
> www.worldwar1.com
> www.channel4.com/history/microsites/F/firstworldwar
> www.greatwar.co.uk
> www.schoolhistory.co.uk/gcselinks/wars/wwi.htm
> www.firstworldwar.com
> www.wikipedia.com

My agent, James Wills of Watson, Little Ltd, suggested, at a very early stage, that the blog could transfer into a successful book. (I do hope he was right . . .) I must thank him for his efforts in finding the right publisher.

At Michael O'Mara Books, Kate Gribble was an earnest and enthusiastic champion of the project. I must recognize the efforts of my editor, Toby Buchan, with his knowledgeable, sensitive and meticulous approach to the task of sorting out this project. Grateful thanks also to Ron Callow of Design 23, and, at Michael O'Mara Books, to Judieth Palmer, Ana Bjezancevic, Anna Marx, Janine Orford, Polly Tingle and Florence Warrington.

Finally, I would like to thank the media (and I'd guess that they don't get this sort of a mention too often . . .). Without the wonderful worldwide publicity for Harry's blog through television, radio, magazines and newspapers, potential readers simply would not have known about it. Indeed, without the publicity, I doubt whether there would have been the incentive to produce this book. In particular, BBC Radio Five Live's *Pods & Blogs* with Chris Vallance first aired the story, following it up with several features on BBC Radio 4's Sunday morning *Broadcasting House* programme. James Roberson of BBC East Midlands spotted the potential for a short TV broadcast which triggered what I can only describe as a media frenzy. I am glad, therefore, to be able to offer my warmest thanks to Chris and James, and to many other journalists or broadcasters who have expressed an interest.

As I have said, I apologize to anyone who feels their name should be here. Any omission is by oversight, and does not in any way lessen either my appreciation, or the value of someone's contribution.

PICTURE ACKNOWLEDGEMENTS

The majority of the illustrations in this book are the author's and, with the exception of those photographs or documents that have appeared on his blog, 'WWI: Experiences of an English Soldier', are published here for the first time.

Grateful thanks to Karl Noble, Collections Officer of the York and Lancaster Regimental Museum, Rotherham, South Yorkshire, for his time and help with illustrations for this book, as well as his expert knowledge (for further information and the museum's address: www.rotherham.gov.uk/graphics/Learning/Museums/EDSYLRM.htm

Thanks are also due to Ray Mentzer of the Great War Primary Document Archive: www.gwpda.org, and to Suzy Blake of the Historic Environment Section of Staffordshire County Council.

The image on page 39 is from *The New Illustrated Encyclopedia* published in the USA by Dodd, Mead and Company. The photograph on page 73 was taken by a Lieutenant J. W. Brooke. The photograph on page 169 is from an Italian book, *Di qua e di là dal Piave. Da Caporetto a Vittorio Veneto (This Side and Over the Piave: From Caporetto to Vittorio Veneto)* by Mario Bernardi, published in 1989 by Mursia Edizione. The photograph on page 173 is also from an Italian book, *Inglesi sull'altopiano (The English on the Plateau)* by Giovanni Cecchin, published in 1995 by Collezione Princeton.

Illustrations other than the author's are from the following sources:

York and Lancaster Regimental Museum, Rotherham: pages 1, 42, 46, 55

Staffordshire County Council: page 26 lower; the plan was drawn by Julian Bagg. Staffordshire CC also supplied the upper image on page 26; with grateful acknowledgement to Jake Whitehouse

First World War Poetry Digital Archive, University of Oxford (www.oucs.ox.ac.uk/wwwLit): page 33; © Imperial War Museum (Q 8435)

Great War Primary Document Archive www.gwpda.org/photo: page 39 upper

National Archive, Kew: pages 48 (WO/95/2188), 75 (WO/95/2188)

Redvers at en.wikipedia (http://en.wikipedia.org): page 79

Popperfoto/Getty Images: page 82

Getty Images: pages 83,

Time & Life Pictures/Getty Images: page 93

AFP/Getty Images: page 194

Mary Evans Picture Library: pages 161, 167

Imperial War Museum: page 170 (Hu 94539)

The medals shown on page 211 are those awarded to Harry Lamin after the end of the Great War.

CHURCH ARMY.

...IVE SERVICE

...FORCE.

Tortona - Ruderi dell'antico forte S. Vittorio

Base.

The following...
signed by the writer:—
I certify on my honour that the...
tents of this envelope refer to nothing...
but private and family matters.

...Signature} W. H. Lam...

very quite...
in a way, not much...
good dinner, We are in...
gnano it is a very...
alley betw...
hen...
not be...
e alrig...
t home...
better f...
gone, ser...
he got av...

Nurse Lamin
Holborn Institution
1 a Shepherdess W...
London N